LETTING GO:
THE WAY INTO ABUNDANCE

The Personal Story of the Founder
of the Beginning Experience

SISTER JOSEPHINE STEWART

CONTENTS

DEDICATION

To Jo Lamia whose journey through grief was the seed of the Beginning Experience and to those, past, present and to come who nurture the growth and maturing of that seed into the vibrant tree that is the Beginning Experience today.

The background of the cover is a watercolor painting named
"Abundance"
by
Sister Josephine Stewart

THANK GOD FOR YOU

My greatest gratitude, aside from my parents, is to you, the Sisters of Saint Mary. Our relationship began in the third grade, when my family moved to Fort Worth, Texas. You taught me the discipline of intense study and of following classroom regulations. What I remember most, however, is Sister Marguerita's kindness. She stayed connected with me throughout the years by writing cards. Then, in high school, I was captured by Sister Mary Margaret's human and understandable approach to sacred mysteries.

After I entered the convent you sent me to Belgium. I was deeply affected by Mother Elizabeth's life. She offered all to God with joy and simplicity. She was my model in her faith journey of letting go of the past and risking new ideas.

I learned from you, Sisters, a balance between discipline and compassion. I learned from you to risk, to let go and to move into the unknown. Your influence became part of my work in creating the Beginning Experience and then in working for its development.

I experienced a call within my vocation as a Sister of Saint Mary to work on behalf of those whose marriages had ended. I felt the same call that our founder, Dom Minsart, must have experienced when, in 1819, he gathered women to help the marginalized people of his time to "leave no need unnoticed." My call was to follow his example and help bring life out of the ashes of death and divorce. That call became a way for me personally to live joyful simplicity and to "leave no need unnoticed."

My prayer life as a Sister of Saint Mary has given me an understanding of the Mystical Christ, which became the underlying theology of the Beginning Experience. Thank you, Sisters, for teaching me to pray. I am especially grateful to Sister Mary Patricia.

I am grateful for the freedom you gave me to pursue the goals of the Beginning Experience, for the freedom you gave me to live with families and to experience life outside of the convent. You trusted me and I trusted you.

I thank the various superiors that I have had who, from time to time, have asked difficult tasks of me. I thank those who were willing to dialog with me and allow new ventures. Above all, I thank the sisters who have lived with and been patient with me. Thank you, Sister Devota, for your constant, prayerful support and work for the Beginning Experience during the last few years in Wichita Falls.

Thank you, Sister Gertrude Moore for showing me how to paint with oils, but most of all how to find joy in painting and in all of life.

Thank you, Sister Cecile Faget, for first suggesting that I write down my stories and then for offering to type my handwritten notes. You actually typed volumes for me to use in writing this book.

Thank you, Sister Ginny Vissing, for reading my manuscript as a Sister of Saint Mary, and making pertinent suggestions about general revisions and Sisters of Saint Mary revisions.

Thank you Sister Clara Vo for your work formatting the sketches and photographs, and for your gentle care of these pages.

Thank you, wonderful people of the Beginning Experience. You have loved and supported me for 35 years.

Thank you, Judith Tate O'Brien, for encouraging me long ago to start the Beginning Experience with your gatherings at Lake Texoma, then for your leadership in the Oklahoma City Beginning Experience, and recently for editing and coaching me in writing and revising this book.

Thank you, Sharon Murphy, for your personal resonance with the chapters as I wrote them, giving me your suggestions and then finding objective readers in California.

Thank you, Dian Hoehne, for your careful editing, proof reading, suggestions and for your prayers.

Thank you, Ann Adams, for your reading as a non-Catholic person who knows and loves me and for making suggestions.

Thank you, Joan Mather, for your affirmations and disagreements with some of my thinking. You gave me thoughtful areas for revision.

Thank you, MaryLee McNeal, for your insightful suggestions of deletions and additions. I am especially grateful for your overview and invitation to focus.

Thank you, Joe Wicker, for giving me peace of mind by taking over the technical end of publishing this book.

Thank you, Lee Prosser, for retrieving my manuscript when I lost it on my computer.

Thank you, Madeline Chappell, for designing the cover and giving it that special look that I insisted on.

And at the end, I thank you, the reader, for selecting my book to read. My prayer is that you will be inspired to search the God in your life and write it down.

FOREWORD

Like thousands of other grieving people, I first came to know of Sister Josephine Stewart as the co-founder of the Beginning Experience® weekend program I attended after my divorce, a program that helped me discover and work through my feelings of pain and loss, and that gave me life, hope and joy again. Like many others, I became a member of my local Beginning Experience team. Through the training I received, and the experience of participating in presenting the program, I came to appreciate even more the power and depth of this special experience.

Like many other team members, I first saw Sister Josephine in person when I attended a Beginning Experience convention, held to educate and communicate with teams about this peer ministry and their special role in it. I remember listening as she told the story of the beginning of the Beginning Experience program. It was a story she told with warmth, humor, and the humility that God had given hurting people this gift through her.

A few years later, I came to know her in person when I joined the Beginning Experience International Board of Directors. I found not only warmth and humor, but a deep love for the people this ministry serves, and Josephine's abundant faith in God's will for it. As founder, she had stepped back by then from a hands-on role, but continued to provide the board with her experience and with a grounding in the ministry's history.

Eventually, I was approached about accepting the role of executive director. Although signs kept coming that this was a path I was being called to follow, I was very hesitant about leaving my job and accepting this role. Conversations with Josephine about risk and having the faith to take this leap helped give me the courage to answer this call. I will always be grateful to her for the rewards I've found in this special way of serving.

The path for this ministry has not always been a smooth or an easy one. In times of crisis, I've witnessed Josephine's strong faith. She talks to God and He answers her with flashes of insight. She has been a very personal blessing not only to this ministry, but to me in my work for it. I know and feel her support and her prayers. Her example and her counsel have helped me in my own personal faith journey as well.

As you read this book, I believe you will find in it a remarkable story and come to know for yourself a remarkable woman. May your life be touched in some way by becoming acquainted with hers. In these pages, may you find an example to follow of letting go, the abundance that can follow from doing so, and the joy to be found in accepting whatever God sends next.

Kathleen Murphy
Executive Director
Beginning Experience International Ministry, Inc.

NOTE:
Beginning Experience® is a registered trademark of Beginning Experience International Ministry, Inc. That registration carries with it certain conventions for the treatment of the words "Beginning Experience" in text. Those conventions are absent in this book, since this is Sister Josephine's personal life story—her memories—written in an informal, conversational style.

INTRODUCTION

This book is the story of the Beginning Experience. It is my story. It is God's story. It is the story of my life intersecting with Jo Lamia's. When my friend, Jo Lamia, told me her story, I heard it and I wrote it down. In Jo's journey through grief, I saw the vision of the Beginning Experience.

These pages disclose the essence of Beginning Experience: to know and love oneself; to pass through, not avoid, pain and grief with Christ who lives within; to receive the gift of trusting in God and to learn to trust in the events of life, in others, and in oneself; to let go of guilt and the past and to forgive the unforgivable; to be fully alive by finishing "unfinished business." In the end they speak of reaching out to others from a heart of compassion. **That–the compassionate reaching out–is the essence of recovery.**

The Beginning Experience taught me to write to God. Eventually I learned to hear His response by writing it down.

The Beginning Experience also gave me the ability to listen. I call it compassionate listening. In writing this book I have tried to listen to people, to events and to God as revealed in my life. As the marvel of Beginning Experience evolved and, I've been blessed to see its beauty in the lives of those who participated in it, I kept asking myself "How and why did God choose me to be his instrument in starting it?"

I found the answer in writing my story. I discovered how God used unlikely elements in my life to create the Beginning Experience. I've also found how He used the Beginning Experience to transform me and countless others. As I reflect on my life through writing, I've discovered the answer to my burning question, "Why did God choose me?" The answer in simple, "Because He wanted to." And I am eternally grateful. I start with my parents' essential contribution to the creation of the Beginning Experience. I continue with the chronological account of my life.

NOTE:
Indication of photographs and sketches appears in the body of the text and refers to APPENDIX 3 where the actual photographs (1-35) are shown or APPENDIX 4 where the actual sketches (A-P) are shown.

CHAPTER 1

IN THE BEGINNING

My Parents

The lives of my parents were precious seeds that grew into the creation of what is known today as the Beginning Experience. My parents lived in the early part of the 20th century, bearing the struggles of their times and learning to adjust to marriage, career and family life. They were Wylie Stewart and Helen Buchanan. Wylie was Presbyterian and Helen was Catholic. My father, Wylie, had experiences that marked his life with loss and feelings of abandonment. At an early age, he lost his mother to the flu epidemic of 1918, which took the lives of countless mothers, fathers and children, in the United States and around the world. Wylie not only witnessed her death, but he reached out to touch her and hold on to her as she was dying. It would be years before I learned more about how his early life had affected him.

Wylie's father remarried after his wife's death and another series of adjustments faced this young man. The relationship with his step-mother was devoid of love and compassion, and he admitted years later that he had actually despised her. One especially painful memory for him was that his stepmother deliberately sold his mother's piano and a special set of China that she had painted.

An even more heart-rending blow for young Wylie was the tragic death of his father a year later. (#1) After Wylie's bout with impetigo and, in an effort to cleanse his son's clothes with gasoline in an old washing machine, Wylie's father was killed when an explosion occurred. How was Wylie to cope with yet another loss?

One tragic event followed another, and Wylie was sent away from home to boarding school. A member of the family told him that it was best to forget his parents and never give them another thought.

These painful events caused deep, deep wounds in my father. Grief, anger and shame became frozen within him, an *unfinishedness* waiting for release.

Wylie matured, attended college and earned a position with Scripps -Howard newspaper in Oklahoma City, and then in El Paso, Texas.

During his years of work in El Paso, Wylie met Helen Buchanan through his association with her brothers, who had come from Lafayette, Louisiana, seeking their livelihoods.

So, Helen Buchanan, the woman who was to be my mother, met my father when she traveled to El Paso to help her divorced sister care for her two children. Helen and her sister were from a large family of eleven children. Helen was already engaged to a man in Lafayette, but her attraction to Wylie led her to break that engagement and marry him, instead, in April of 1930.

Helen was the last child born to Josephine (#2) and John Charles Buchanan. John Charles had served in the Confederacy in the Civil War and spent most of the war as a prisoner. He died when Helen was two years old and so she, too, experienced the loss of a parent. She had no memory at all of her father.

My mother had been surrounded by women in the Buchanan family during her childhood. She was always fashionably dressed, looking lovely in her outfits, the latest flapper-style dresses made especially for her by her older sister. However, the skills usually handed down to women in those days, of cooking, sewing and housekeeping, were sorely lacking in Helen's upbringing. Furthermore, a solid down-to-earth preparation for marriage and family life was simply absent in Helen's formation.

Wedding outfits of a navy serge suit and flower trimmed wedding dress adorned the young couple. (#s 3 and 4) A honey-moon excursion in Wylie's Buick Roadster, led them down unpaved roads toward Houston–interrupted by one flat tire–and then on to Lafayette to meet the Buchanan relatives. Helen's mother, who herself had been married to a Presbyterian, approved of Wylie. Then, the second leg of the trip began to the Stewart family in Oklahoma to seek the approval of his side of the family. Mama got her period on the trip and she was miserable. Daddy was aghast, knowing next-to-nothing about the cycles in women's lives. Those were sensitive issues for the young couple in those times.

So an industrious and hard-working individual, Wylie Stewart, bearing the wounds of loss, tragedy and abandonment began a life wedded to Helen, a naive, inexperienced young woman, quite un-prepared for homemaking and motherhood. Helen's oldest sister was heard to remark, God help those two babes in the wood. And, of course, God did. The combination of unfinishedness in them was exactly what God used in their life and in mine. **The Beginning Experience, with its emphasis on passing through grief, found its early roots in my parents, in their struggles and their survival.**

My Birth and First Months in El Paso

Now that both sides of the family approved, even embraced, their new in-laws, married life began in earnest for Mama and Daddy.

Grandma Buchanan wrote to Mama every Sunday. Her witty comments in both French and English depicted the adventures of the Buchanans. In addition she gave the kind of guidance that Mama desperately needed, especially during her pregnancy with me. Grandma was passionate about writing Mama, her youngest daughter, explaining how to proceed through the unknown wilderness of pregnancy. In one letter she explained how to oil the stretch marks.

These weekly letters from 1929 to 1958 still exist in two leather bound volumes, a Christmas gift from Daddy to Mama. These volumes became a living history of our family and served as a major source of information for me.

Daddy worked very hard at the newspaper in El Paso proving himself to have settled down. On occasion he brought a guest home for dinner. One time the stew contained (heaven forbid!) unpeeled potatoes and even a nail which somehow had fallen into the pot. After that Mama was the brunt of many jokes which hurt her feelings.

I was born October 12, 1931. Mama had a hard, painful, 36-hour labor. I was pretty banged up from being in the birth canal so long, and daddy cried when he saw me. I believe that I became a survivor because of the ordeal of being born. I turned out to be a beautiful baby. (#5)

My mother named me after Grandma, Josephine Eugenie. And because Mama had a huge devotion to Saint Joseph as patron of everything, it was important to name me her first born after him. Her devotion stemmed from the fact that Joseph was the earthly father of Jesus. That meant she could count on him to personally care for her as he had for Jesus and Mary. My hunch is that since she did not know her own father, Saint Joseph became a symbol of a father for her.

Because Daddy was so involved in a complicated assignment at the newspaper, Uncle John took special care of Mama and me. He was like a father to Mama because when Mama was little after her father's death, and John was still at home on the farm, he had cared for her playing with her and loving her. Then he had gone off to World War I. When the war was over he had moved to El Paso. In looking back, God's plan becomes clearer by putting him in Mama's life at a critical time.

During all that time Grandma continued writing to Mama every week, giving her advice. Mama must have written to her explaining that she had weaned me at three months, according to the instructions in a little black book and that I was screaming all the time. The instructions advised that mothers should not pick up their screaming babies. Grandma wrote to Mama that she should throw away the little black book and pick me up. Mama didn't know what to do because by then I was furiously sucking my thumb. She put metal caps on my hands to keep me from doing that. I was a frustrated and angry baby, and Mama had no rest because of my screaming.

Meanwhile the time in El Paso was coming to an abrupt end. Daddy's work at the newspaper involved him in a dangerous episode uncovering some illegal gambling in El Paso. When gangsters threatened his life, he left on three days notice, for Oklahoma City. He drove the Buick Roadster over unpaved roads and spent one night in a room that was so dirty that he put newspapers on the bed.

To join him, Mama packed everything up and took the train to Oklahoma City. I was six months old. The trip must have been horrible with me screaming and being inconsolable. To add to her pain, when she unpacked she found that all her precious Haviland wedding china had been broken. That was the final blow for her! With that loss, and leaving Uncle John, she had to say good bye to the past and look to Daddy's family in Oklahoma City. The Stewarts loved her and brought her into the family. There she found great support in Daddy's Aunt Bessie, (#6) and Daddy returned to his dear cousin and best friend, Coonie. It was a new start for them.

4

CHAPTER 2

MY CHILDHOOD AND ADOLESCENCE

When I was 18 months old, my brother Mack was born in Oklahoma City. Daddy was proud of a boy. My brother's arrival was too much for me to let go of being Number One. I was distraught and sometimes even hit little Mack in his crib. Daddy often angrily scolded me. I remember feeling a lot of shame and holding my head down. Mama was often sick with bad headaches. I learned to take care of her, comfort her, and bring her favorite drink, pear juice. Mama referred to me as Jonie, the name Mack gave me because he couldn't pronounce Josephine.

When I was four years old, I got pneumonia and was taken to a hospital. They told me later that I almost died. Mama's best friend, Betsy, brought me one of her antique china dolls. I really disliked Betsy, because Mama spent too much time with her and she called me "silly." When she handed me the beautiful doll, I flung it across the room and broke it into pieces. Mama fussed at me and then she and Betsy left. I felt a lot of shame. I was afraid and alone. The nurse came in and took care of me. Later, Aunt Bessie came and held me and told me everything would be all right, but I had stored up negative feelings of shame.

Meanwhile, Mama continued to receive weekly letters from Grandma. The most interesting during this period of time was advice on how to avoid getting pregnant. Mama had apparently written saying that she did not want any more children at that time. Grandma consulted with Nannie and sent her instructions on the "Rhythm Method" of abstaining during one's fertile period.

I attended pre-school when I was four. (#7) That seemed all right, but when it was time for first grade, I was not ready and I couldn't cope. I was afraid of being separated from Mama and I vomited every morning and she often kept me home. As a result I failed First

Grade. I continued to suck my thumb well into the second year of First Grade.

Sometime, in the ensuing years, Mama matured. I no longer thought of her as helpless and needing to be cared for. She became strong and able to speak out. She had great faith. After her death, I found her book, *Rebuilding a Lost Faith*, by John L. Stoddard. I believe that Grandma had sent her the book along with the "Rhythm Method" to help her in her arduous life.

For years, Daddy always seemed angry. He worked long hours and was disgusted with his co-workers at the newspaper. The newspaper was, in Mama's words, "a den of iniquity." She prayed fervently, imploring Saint Joseph to do something. My sister, Catharine, was born during that turmoil, six years after Mack. So the "Rhythm Method" had worked.

Saint Joseph arranged for the newspaper in Oklahoma City to go bankrupt. But he also arranged to re-locate Daddy and his growing family to Fort Worth, Texas. That made it possible for Daddy to work within the same company, Scripps-Howard Newspapers.

It was thus that we moved, in April 1939, to Fort Worth, so that Daddy could work at The Press. Catharine was six months old when we moved. I attended public school for the short end of that school year. Ultimately Mama insisted on a Catholic education for us. She went to the nuns and arranged for a reduction. Daddy never really understood her passion for a Catholic education. He thought it was inferior to public education and that the old Catholic school building was ugly and inadequate. I just remember there was a great deal of tension between Mama and Daddy.

In the fall, Mack and I started at Saint Mary's School. He was in the first grade and I was in the third grade. I have happy memories of a tall, tall priest, Father Herbert, who taught us religion. He was a marvelous influence of gentleness for me then and throughout my life.

Mama prayed a lot. Every evening, we said the rosary. Mama, Mack, Catharine and I knelt. Daddy remained walled off behind his newspaper. Mama would start, "In the name of the Father and of the Son and of the Holy Ghost–for the conversion of Wylie Stewart." The newspaper never moved, nor did he become Catholic until I was in college.

We grew up during World War II. I have indelible memories of December 7, 1941, the bombing of Pearl Harbor. We went to our friends, the Herndons, and listened to the news on the upright Philco Radio. I was ten. I remember feeling afraid of the Japanese and the Nazis. Mama had a way of getting our fear and anger out. She made bread and had us knead the bread by pounding it as though we were punching Hitler and Hiro Hito.

We did our part for the war effort. We raised rabbits and had "fried rabbit" instead of fried chicken for Sunday dinner. Meat, sugar, gasoline and shoes were all rationed. Each family got ration stamps. We had a "Victory Garden" on the corner vacant lot. We went most evenings, spring and summer, weeding and harvesting the crops. Since no one had a freezer Mama canned the green beans, onions, squash, okra, corn and tomatoes. Mack and I had a little vegetable stand in our front yard to sell our surplus. We learned to be creatively frugal.

Daddy found a stray dog and brought him home. Mack and I were in one of our big fights but when we saw this beautiful little Collie we stopped fighting to play with him. Mama named him Chris, after Saint Christopher, because he had saved the day. Chris became our best friend, following us to school every morning, staying outside at the school during the day and then coming home with us in the afternoon.

On April 19, 1943, this beloved Collie was killed running after our car as we returned from the Victory Garden. I remember kneeling next to his lifeless body and begging God to bring him back to life. I cried bitterly and kept saying, "If only we had let him in the car." I felt so guilty that we could have prevented his death. This was the first big loss in my life. I took a long time to heal from the sadness and the guilt feelings. I still feel the sadness.

Since it was very hot and there was no such thing as air-conditioning we all slept in our screened front porch. We kids were on mattresses on the floor and Mama and Daddy were on canvas army cots. That worked out well.

One night a man was chasing Mack. Mama was very pregnant, but she walked to the side door where the man stood and said in a loud, firm voice, "In the name of Jesus Christ, leave my son alone." The man ran away.

In High School, (#8) I had a wonderful teacher, Sister Mary Margaret. She explained the Trinity and the Incarnation to us in a way that I understood.

About the Trinity she told us that in eternity the Father speaks a Word. This Word contains His whole and entire Being. He loves this Word, the Son; and this Word loves Him back. Their mutual Love is the Holy Spirit.

About the Incarnation, she explained that the Father and the Son made the decision that the Son would become a human being. This meant that He would be both God and human. It meant that He would never use His Divine Power to rescue Himself from the cruelty of people against Him. Her explanation stayed with me, knowing the extent of Jesus' vulnerability in His human nature.

I'm sure that Sister Mary Margaret did not realize that I would keep her words in my heart and that they would be a rock of understanding for my whole life.

It was when I was in Sister Mary Margaret's class that Charlie was born. Mama had Catharine board at Our Lady of Victory so that she could devote her energies to Charlie. Later Catharine told me that she felt left out, but that Daddy gave her a supply of nickels to call him every afternoon at his office. She did not like the boarding school food and lost a lot of weight.

I became Charlie's second mother, caring for him, diapering, feeding and playing with him. But mostly I observed in awe the development of this precious baby brother. When I left within the year for college Catharine took over being his other mother.

Growing up in Fort Worth in the 1940's was an adventure in independence. My brother, Mack, and I rode everywhere on the bus. We didn't depend on anyone to take us where we wanted to go. We walked to the movies on Saturday afternoon and saw whatever was playing and the cartoon and Pathe News. The cost was ten cents.

With our independence, we asked Mama if we could take Charlie (three months old) for a ride on the bus. She didn't hesitate to say yes. So Mack, Catharine and I got on the bus with Charlie. He was dressed in his best blue, knit sweater outfit. We transferred once to get to the photographer where we had our individual portraits made. Mama never asked us where we had been. The black and white panel of portraits was our Christmas gift to Mama and Daddy.

These are just some of the highlights of my growing up. The birth of Charlie and Sister Mary Margaret's teaching had a huge impact on my life. **I can see the seeds that God cultivated in me that eventually had something to do with the creation of the Beginning Experience. Several points stand out: Daddy's anger, my feeling abandoned when I was weaned and when I had pneumonia, my caring for Mama and her devotion to Saint Joseph, my feelings of fear during the war, my grief and guilt over the death of our beloved dog, my outspoken nature as the oldest, my love of God and understanding of the Trinity and Incarnation, and my independent nature.**

In writing these memoirs, I have become aware of the threads in my life that became part of the Beginning Experience. Two such threads are the sense of early shame, at having broken the doll, and my sensitivity to the tension caused by the arguing between my parents about Catholic education. Perhaps as a result I included in the Beginning Experience: facing guilt and forgiving oneself, and communication skills. (See Appendix: What Is the Beginning Experience?)

CHAPTER 3

THE CORNERSTONE OF MY LIFE

Leaving Home, College, Teaching and Entering the Convent

I graduated with honors from Our Lady of Victory Academy in May of 1948. Mama and Daddy wanted to send me to college, but money was very scarce. Aunt Sally and Uncle Paul asked me to come live with them and attend the college in Lafayette, Louisiana. That college, Southwestern Louisiana Institute, was very dear to the Buchanan family. Nannie taught math there and almost all of my cousins had attended. Mama had worked for the Dean of Women as a stenographer before going to El Paso. But most importantly, my grandfather had designed the first buildings of the college.

I was delighted to accept this wonderful offer and so I enrolled at S.L.I. in September 1948. Nannie introduced me to Tico from Brazil, one of her math students. Tico and I went to the Freshman Dance and continued dating for two years. Aunt Sally and Uncle Paul became his family. He showered me with gifts. He came home with me at Christmas and Mama dearly loved him.

My favorite activity was being on the Red Jackets drill team. We traveled with the team to their football games, performing precision routines. I was in the Biology Club which gave me another opportunity to go on adventures in the Gulf of Mexico and in the marsh lands and swamps. I spent more time having fun than studying, but maintained good grades.

The Newman Club at the Catholic Student Center introduced me to a wise and holy priest who took time to guide us students and who became a good friend.

After Tico transferred to the state university in Baton Rouge, I fell in love several times. I loved to dance to the big bands that came to our college. Jitterbugging was my favorite. I sewed all my evening dresses.

Despite my involvement at school, I returned home every noon hour. Noon dinner was quite a family tradition. Monday and

Thursday all the Buchanans left work or school and gathered at Aunt Sally and Uncle Paul's; on Tuesdays, they all came to Grandma's; and Wednesdays they all went to Aunt Virginia's. These meals were extraordinary, made from "scratch" and using fresh vegetables and three selections of fresh meat. Nannie's lemon meringue pie was outstanding as was Aunt Sally's baked custard. Uncle Paul always ate his dessert first. He was spoiled by Aunt Sally. After dinner, he took a little nap in his chair and at 1:30 returned to his dentist office right there on the property.

I loved our big family and all the gatherings. Aunt Sally and Uncle Paul had no children of their own and generously provided home for many of us in this extended family. They gave us all unconditional, real human love, wisdom, humor and safety.

Grandma Buchanan was an important influence in my life. Since her husband's death, when my mother was two, she always wore the same-style black shirtwaist dress. But more than anything she showed courage and faith. Being descended from the exiled Acadians of Canada, she spoke with a heavy French accent. She was a true Cajun (the shortened name for Acadians).

Her philosophy was summed up when she said "If I had been a pagan, I would have worshipped the sun." She was a sun person–very positive and joyful. She went to daily Mass at Mount Carmel Convent behind her house. She lived with Auntie (Josephine), Nannie (Ann) who taught math, and "Uncle" Sophy, who said there were too many Aunts (eight of them) in the family, so she dubbed herself "Uncle."

Every evening at 7:00, they prayed the rosary. Aunt Sally and Aunt Virginia joined them. I came often. The heavy fragrance of magnolias and gardenias and the smell of the wide beamed cypress floors is still with me.

Uncle Sophy was a bit eccentric. She worked for Hadacol (Happy Day Company of Lafayette). She slept year round on the screened-in back porch. She loved her Arabian horse "more than people." She was very funny and had a mischievous twinkle in her dark eyes. She danced magnificently. She was two years older than Mama. When she and Mama were still at home, Auntie sewed beautiful flapper style dresses for them.

I was very blessed to have spent my college years with Mama's family. Their influence on my life was profound. I felt deep in my soul the married love of Aunt Sally and Uncle Paul, a love that spilled over to everyone in humble giving to those in need and to our family. I cherished that love even more because they were so unselfconscious about it. They appeared to express love effortlessly. I never heard them angry at one another. They slept holding each other in a huge Victorian carved bed.

When I graduated, (#9) I wanted to work in my field of Clothing and Design. After a short beach vacation in Biloxi, my friend Elaine and I went to Dallas to seek employment at Neiman Marcus. Elaine left abruptly after being unsettled by two encounters with brothels in Dallas which came about when we were searching for an apartment. In the first incident the "landlady" thought we were applying to be "ladies of the night." So we went across town and found another apartment and it was the same there. I didn't take that seriously, but Elaine decided to return to Lafayette.

I lived with Mama and Daddy, who had moved to north Dallas, and I worked at Neiman Marcus. The atmosphere there was one of sexual harassment and intimidation. I just remember always worrying about something: selling enough to get a decent commission, fending off men with their propositions, and always feeling very uncomfortable with that workplace in the "fast track."

I worked on the famous September "Fortnight" style show. The day the "Fortnight" closed, Sister Mary Brigid, who had been my high school principal, called me from Fort Worth to see if I would consider coming to teach Home Economics at Our Lady of Victory Academy. I jumped at the chance to get out of "hell on earth." I don't recall that I gave any notice to Neiman Marcus. I was clearly not suited for working there.

And so, in October of 1952, I went to O.L.V. as Miss Stewart, teaching Home Ec. to high school girls and college students and nutrition to Saint Joseph's Hospital nursing students. I lived in a room across the street and took my meals with the college students, most of whom were barely four years younger than I was. Dear Sister Eleanor, who had been my beloved freshman teacher, was the principal. She taught me a lot about how to teach. But more than that, I saw her heroism during her struggle with cancer. She lost an eye that year.

At Easter time one of my old boyfriends came to see me. His attention to me and wishing to pursue a deeper relationship frightened me. I had not considered marrying him and was faced with giving him an answer. I was very confused about my feelings and so I told him I intended to enter the convent.

After having told him that lie, I felt obligated to go through with trying out the convent. I reasoned that marriage is until "death do us part," but that I could enter the convent and then I'd have plenty of time to decide about the "death do us part" idea. I knew that I could enter the novitiate and then decide. Why did I use the convent as the escape hatch in my confusion? I think that on a subliminal level I was thinking of both Sister Mary Margaret's and Sister Eleanor's impact on my spiritual life.

After an adventurous family vacation in the undeveloped area of Platora and Crested Butte in Colorado, I got the mumps. I stayed in bed in Dallas until I entered the convent on August 6, Feast of the Transfiguration, 1953.

Even though I was still unsure about having a vocation, I took the habit of the Sisters of Saint Mary and became Sister Raphael. That name honored someone I loved–the Archangel Raphael, patron of healing and happy encounters. In the Old Testament, the angel Raphael led Tobit to find the fish oil for healing his father's blindness and then guided him to find his wife Sarah.

I felt a lot of guilt about being with the other novices who seemed so holy and sure of God's will. But then came another moment of decision, when my superiors decided that I would go to Namur, Belgium, to make my novitiate. No American sister had gone to our mother house since World War II. I agonized (I did have some conscience) over whether I should tell the sisters that I wasn't sure of staying, or whether I should take that European trip about which I'd always dreamed.

I said nothing and, in the spring, I left for Belgium. I remember sitting in Dulles Airport in Washington, DC thinking "I've lied to the sisters," and feeling guilty about going to Europe under false pretenses.

Namur was like a storybook with its Citadel on the hill, its cobblestone streets and quaint buildings. My indecision began to melt.

The novitiate building, located at the top of a hill overlooking Namur, was filled with young novices from around the world. (#10) Our confessor, Père Standard, came every Thursday afternoon and he spoke English. The first time I went and knelt down to confess, I unloaded all the guilt I was feeling about lying to the sisters to get to come to Belgium. I'll never forget his reaction. He chuckled and said, "My precious child, just relax and let go now, and let God work in your life." And that is what I did. "Relax and let God work" became a motto for my life.

That was the turning point. I had this wonderful, understanding priest to talk to in English. I was even assigned to serve him coffee and cookies after confessions. He truly became my spiritual father. **He helped me see that God could and would take away all my fears and guilt, if I let go, and trusted Him to lead me on His way, despite my mistakes.**

Life in the novitiate was both joyful and harsh, preparing the novices for whatever assignments they would have in the future. Many were destined for foreign missions. I remember the most demanding work was the laundry.

We novices did the laundry with primitive equipment, especially for the 1950's. We put the clothes in a large copper cylinder full of soapy water. Using the handles on either side, we tumbled it over and over, above a coal fire. After this washing process we put the clothes into cold water in a huge cement vat. Next, we put the white clothes out on the lush green grass and sprinkled them with salt to bleach in the sun. After this bleaching, all the clothes went back to a second vat of cold water. We rinsed them until they were free of soap and salt and then hung them on the lines to dry. The laundry included all white clothes, towels, bed linens and kitchen cloths. This was a huge weekly task, taking from early morning until supper time, stopping only for prayers. My hands were raw from this painful process, but then I considered this due penance for my sins.

In order to learn French, I was enrolled in Namur, in the sixth grade to learn dictation. This meant that three times a week I walked twelve miles–three miles down the hill to our mother house, three miles up the hill for lunch, three miles down the hill for afternoon classes and three miles back up the hill at the end of the day. Marathon walking was nothing for the Belgian sisters, but it was mammoth for me. The pounds did come off and I did learn French quickly. After about six months I could understand everything and even dreamed in French.

On the joyful side, I went to art class in Huy. My teacher was Soeur Agnes Marie. She was always smiling. She had "la joie de vivre." Her mother, having entered as a widow, was also in our order. Soeur Agnes Marie showed me how to make intricate designs and balance forms in various spaces: squares, circles, triangles, pentagons and hexagons. I learned the essentials of design and balance under her loving and patient tutoring. I used drafting equipment and carefully painted in my designs with India ink using a flat nosed pen. A thread that wove itself through my life was my love for art and my skill in designing beautiful drawings and paintings.

I looked forward to the Wednesday excursions on the bus to Huy. The bus was filled with interesting folk: workers and families who boarded the bus along the way.

As an art student, I also attended Saint Giles art school in Brussels to learn ceramics, from a master teacher. Part of the students' curriculum was a trip to "far away places" in the art world. I went with these students once to Rotterdam, which had been destroyed in the war, and Amsterdam. We studied on location the Flemish masters and had guided tours of the marvelous museums and churches. On another student trip we went to the World War I battlefields in France and saw many restored churches. I wasn't cloistered in that novitiate. On the contrary all the novices experienced a lot to expand their education and vision.

We walked everywhere. We attended the Jesuit University on Thursday evenings for classes where we received a broad theological background. My time in Belgium was right before Vatican II and the Belgian church was way ahead of the American church in the realm of renewal. Already Mass was in French instead of Latin and we said the Divine Office (the monastic prayers of the church) in French.

The finest part of my spiritual development was the instruction of our dear Mother Elisabeth. She visited us at the novitiate and explained how to be Sisters of Saint Mary. She motivated us to live our motto "In the simplicity of my heart, I have joyfully offered all to the Lord." She and all the Belgian sisters had lived through World War II. She was novice mistress during the war. She had many harrowing stories to tell of moving all the novices to safety in France. The Germans were hiding in our novitiate buildings and the Americans were bombing our buildings to destroy the Germans. She spoke with lived authority about the war times. I admired her.

16

She was responsible for the forward-looking changes in our order long before Vatican II. She was a risk taker. She was both holy and down to earth. I often thanked God for "my happy fault" that got me to Belgium which influenced my whole life. I began to be honest with myself and to sort out fears, guilt and shame, and to let go.

I also became attached to my sisters in the novitiate and dreaded leaving this safe cocoon and returning to the real world. Anticipatory grief brought a cloud over the last few months there. I was blessed to talk with Père Standard who had been a missionary and who knew the sadness of letting go and leaving people.

Some other aspects of the novitiate were a challenge for me. These experiences were easy for the Belgian sisters but were difficult and exhausting for me. We cleaned the coal storage area under the cobblestone courtyard until our white veils and faces became black. We whitewashed the interior church walls. We unstitched the mattresses, spread the horsehair stuffing out on the grass, cleaned them, and then sewed them back in the covers. It seemed like I was there for the "every-few-years-we-do-this" tasks. I learned a lot. We kept the novitiate buildings, the front stoop and walkway, and church spotless like all good women in Belgium. We even wore wooden shoes for some of the work.

Christmas is a memory that sums up my novitiate experience. After the silence of Advent, and after midnight Mass, we went into the refectory. My heart skipped as I beheld such glowing beauty. The walls were punctuated with dozens of beautiful little shelf decorations. Each one held a tiny burning candle, giving a soft glow to the room. Music was playing, "Jesu, Joy of Man's Desiring." The tables were decorated with delightful Christmas ornamentations and on them were the famous Belgian log cakes like the ones we saw in bakery shop windows down in Namur. The surprise and the exquisite beauty of this experience was like a vision of love–an imprint of the Incarnation–the Word made flesh.

Somehow through my novitiate, everything began to make sense to me: the world, the beauty of nature, spirituality, self honesty, God's closeness and friendship, and those loving wonderful nuns. I felt a serenity that warmed my soul. I never wanted that to end. It was the Camelot period of my religious life.

We often sang in harmony, beautiful songs in French. One became the theme song of my life and I still sing it often. "Seigneur, mon ami, tu m'a pris par la main. J'irais avec toi sans efroi jusqu'au but du chemin. Tra la la la la la" "Lord, my friend, you have taken me by the hand. I will go with you without fear even to the end of the road."

I pronounced my first vows of poverty, chastity and obedience as a Sister of Saint Mary of Namur, on February 2, 1957, in the beautiful church of the novitiate. The stained glass crucifix behind the altar had already been emblazoned in my heart from many times of prayer in this church. Père Standard, my friend, gave the homily about the vows nailing me to the cross of Christ. I felt very holy and whole, and very dedicated to a life of sacrifice for the kingdom. The first sacrifice I felt was leaving Belgium and the nuns to whom I had become attached. I cried and then I felt guilty about crying. I was leaving home. **Letting go was necessary for me in order to go on with the rest of my life and to experience God's abundance.**

CHAPTER 4

ORDINARY TIMES AND DESERT TIMES

Teaching, OLV Superior, BDHS Principal, Guidance Counselor

My two years in Belgium in the novitiate and the painful letting go for my re-entry into reality, gave me a foundation for my religious life. **I had learned that God's power held me, that I could trust Him to bring good out of my mistakes, that He loved me unconditionally, that He would direct me into His will, and that I could live through difficult situations because of his grace.**

Immediately, this trust was put to the test, when I was sent to Texas, in February 1957, for my first teaching job as a nun. I was 26 years old. I was assigned to teach freshmen girls at Our Lady of Good Counsel Academy (L.G.C.) in Oak Cliff in Dallas. Their beloved teacher was leaving in the middle of the year. Those girls loved her, almost adored her. They were very sad at her leaving and they were very resistant to my coming. They were a mischievous bunch anyway, and they made my life miserable.

Even though I had been a teacher prior to entering the convent, somehow I lost all that teaching ability in Belgium. I remember, tearfully, pleading with Sister Justin. She was the seasoned, calm principal. She deftly guided me through that first half year and I re-learned how to teach.

The next year my joy for teaching deepened. I taught 48 freshmen girls upstairs in the old convent of L.G.C. Fun loving talented girls occupied eight rows of large wooden desks. They were a delight to teach even when they played pranks on me.

Patty Ridgley, a wonderful student, full of mischief, put something in my top drawer and asked me to get a pencil out. There was a live, long, squirming worm. She admitted she was not alone in the plot, so I told the whole class to tell their parents that the next day they would stay in for an hour. The next day came, and they all stayed in detention. I let them out at 4:00 April 2, 1958, at the exact moment when the historic Dallas tornado hit Oak Cliff. That meant that all of my 48 students were out on the streets of Oak Cliff, at bus stops or walking home. I stood outside our convent and watched the tornado, roaring like a train, skipping around our neighborhood.

I was praying that God would make all things right, as He always had for me. No one was harmed. *Life Magazine* had a big spread on this tornado. And I never, ever again kept a class in detention.

I loved teaching and loved my students. I was the Sodality moderator. The Sodality was an extra-curricular organization that aided the spiritual growth of its members. I was the spiritual advisor for the Sodalists. At that time we used the Young Christian Students' process of "See, Judge, and Act" which taught reflecting on situations, especially social situations, discerning what to do, and then acting on the discernment. The Sodalists kept logs of their spiritual growth and met with me regularly. This was a powerful spiritual formation for these young hearts.

Together, on Fridays after school, we went to a nearby poor nursing home. What an experience we all had, listening to these elders and sprinkling a bit of youthful joy!

After my grace-filled years at L.G.C., I was appointed, at age 30, to be Superior of our mother house, Our Lady of Victory. I was petrified, sick, unsure, scared and obedient.

This large, five story brick building, on Hemphill Street in Fort Worth was where I had attended high school and where I had taught Home Ec. But on that day when I arrived to become the Superior, it looked monstrous and foreboding. It had become the enemy. I remember praying the psalm that starts, "Out of the depths I cry to you, O Lord." I think I was the youngest professed sister in the house. I'm not sure of this. My view was distorted. Some let me know quite soon that they were older and wiser than me. This was the desert–a "dry weary land without water."

The high school classes had just moved to the new diocesan school, but the high school boarders still lived there and were driven to classes every day. The elementary school boarders also lived there. The convent was filled with retired and infirmed sisters. The sisters who taught at the parish schools in Fort Worth lived there, as well as the novices and novice mistress. What an assortment of people! All of them, except me, knew exactly what to do.

The infirmed sisters needed nursing care and there was no organized infirmary yet. Some of us learned to give injections by practicing on an orange. The actual administering of injections was the hardest thing I ever did.

That year, five sisters died. I had never been with anyone who was dying. I remember being very afraid. The spirituality of that era, the early 60's, was white knuckle obedience. I had faith, sprinkled with doubting, that God would come through when He asked the impossible.

In time, death and dying became familiar to me. Actually I often meditated on Jesus' suffering, death and resurrection. My former high school principal, Sister Mary Brigid, died that year. However, at the moment of her death, I was out in the yard tending to the infestation of bag worms on our cedar trees. I felt guilty that I had left her side to take care of a physical aspect of my job.

The passing of these five sisters made a lasting impression on me. That year became for me a deeper trusting of God to bring goodness out of chaos, but deep inside of me I had conflict between trusting and profound doubting.

I really needed the gift of trust because in August, I was sent to be principal of the girls' division of Bishop Dunne High School in Oak Cliff, Dallas. (#11) The Brothers of the Sacred Heart came to teach the boys. It was the new diocesan co-institutional high school that had come from the old L.G.C. Since I knew the students and parents, my superiors thought I'd be a good choice. But I did not know how to be a principal. I felt very inadequate. In contrast, Brother Martin who was principal of the boys' division was a formidable, experienced principal. I literally quaked when I heard his booming voice.

I muddled along for two years in this job for which I was not suited. I made innumerable mistakes. I felt adrift, abandoned by both God and my superiors. I was angry and I questioned.

Two death experiences stand out. The first was the assassination of President Kennedy, November 22, 1963. Our senior girls had been bussed to the parade and had seen the president moments before he was shot. Several of our seniors were to have helped serve the banquet at the Trade Center. One of them had the presence of mind to bring me the yellow roses from the head table. I made memorial cards with these petals. I used the quotation from Isaiah that was in Kennedy's speech that morning. It was about "setting the captives free." The subsequent events surrounding his tragic death, his sorrowful funeral and Jack Ruby's bizarre shooting of Oswald at the Dallas Police Station are still emblazoned in my memory.

The other memory of death was of one of our students. We had dismissed early for Christmas vacation and the students were in high spirits. The young woman who was killed had actually gotten on the city bus to go home. A friend called to her to get off the bus. I'm not sure exactly how the accident happened, but at a curve, their speeding car broke through the guard rail of the freeway and landed on a truck below, killing an elderly African American man as well as our student. The police officers brought me her gray uniform jacket which still had her bus transfer stub in its pocket. Her funeral was a sad and sobering experience for every student and for us, the faculty.

Along with Sister Patricia Ridgley, my former student who was teaching at Dunne High School, I attended the funeral and burial of the elderly man. It was a moving dramatization of the events leading up to his sudden death and it revealed that community's vivid expression of their anguish and pain.

There were also many funny events. They provided some comic relief from an otherwise very serious daily grind.

Every day I smelled smoke as I walked down the ramp in front of Father Tim's counseling office. I had opened the door to his waiting room several times, but never found anything. One day I was determined to solve the mystery. I sniffed around and discovered that the smell of smoke was coming from the air conditioning storage area. I opened the door to discover two of our girls sitting on the floor smoking. I stood in silence above them, ominous in my long black habit. When they left, there was a puddle. One of them had wet on the floor.

The divisive wave in our country during the 60's was evident in our girls. Our students came long distances by school bus. The buses were clearly marked "BISHOP DUNNE CATHOLIC HIGH SCHOOL." I did not know how long the rude behavior on the bus had been going on until the day I received a phone call from a non-Catholic man. He explained that the girls on the back of the bus stood up at every stop light and mooned the cars behind. In my naiveté I, along with the parents was in disbelief. The PTA took up the matter.

Another time, I was in the chapel and heard strange groaning sounds coming from the confessional. When I opened the door and found a boy and girl making out, her response shocked me. "Sister Raphael, what I do with my ass is my business, not yours."

Our community of sisters was delightful. The oldest member was Sister Ferdinand, originally from Massachusetts; she spoke with a strong Boston accent. She had visited Bishop T. K. Gorman's home and came back with two baby ducks. We named them Tee and Kay after the Bishop. They lived in the girls' patio surrounded by classrooms. Tee and Kay increased and multiplied. Their mating was great entertainment during algebra and other classes. Every year, there were yellow fluffs waddling after Kay and swimming in the tiny pond in the middle of the patio.

We were all attached to the duck families. One morning we discovered duck feathers strewn all over the patio, but no ducks. The precious ducks had apparently been devoured by some beast. We hurried to tell Father Tim about this tragedy and he and Brother Carl came to see what the matter could be. Father Tim and Brother Carl were great friends and fishing buddies. They started laughing. "Don't you see? There's no blood. We took an old stuffed duck and spread the feathers all over to play a joke on you." They certainly succeeded.

We sisters had a puppy named Antigone, Tig for short. Sister Ferdinand spoiled her with chocolates. One Friday afternoon when our confessor came, Sister Ferdinand was rushing to go to confession and she tripped over Tig and broke her shoulder. I was afraid to tell our provincial that Tig was the cause of the accident, so I made up another story. I was afraid that we'd have to give Tig away, and that would cause us psychological damage in addition to Sister Ferdinand's broken shoulder. When Tig grew up she thought she was a nun. She would race around the convent patio with the burlap sack (her blanket) on her head like a veil.

Sister Marie Josephine (not me) was a dynamic religion teacher and a tall regal woman. One morning about six o'clock, she leaned against the sink in her bedroom and broke it off the wall. Cascades of water flowed from her room into the hall and down the stairs. We finally got the water turned off and using every towel and mop we had, wrung out all the water. Then we marched over to the chapel for Mass. Father Beaumont was our visiting priest that day. The first reading was about Moses striking the rock and the water gushing out. We not only giggled, we laughed uncontrollably. It wasn't until after Mass that we could explain our hysteria.

My two year tenure as Principal was not all fun and games. I detested the job and begged to be relieved of an assignment for which I was ill-suited. My plea was heard and I stepped down to be assistant principal, which was much better for me and the students. (#12)

I felt relaxed in my job as assistant principal. In the spring, I became aware that several of the senior boys were getting into trouble their last few months before graduation. I suggested that a Senior Play might capture their interest and therefore ensure their graduation. Brother Adrian, the new principal of the boys' division liked the idea. A teacher from Jesuit high school directed the play. He chose *She Stoops to Conquer*, a rather complicated play. We asked these mischievous boys to try out for the play. The son's part went to Kevin Lamia and the father's part went to a popular African American student. I overheard them questioning how this could work out. Kevin said, "We'll just say, 'I is adopted.'"

At the climax of the play, Kevin sat on the couch so hard it crashed backwards. The audience went wild. Kevin was the son of Jo Lamia, who later became the co-founder of the Beginning Experience. She reported to me that Kevin recited all the parts of the play every day. He knew the whole play by heart and so did she. The play united our senior class, was a huge success, was held over–and all the boys graduated.

At some point during this time, I stopped wearing the habit and took back my given name, Josephine. I went from being assistant principal to being guidance counselor, a position that I really loved. (#13)

I did personal counseling with students as well as academic, college and job selection counseling. And I worked with scheduling. In the summer, prior to school, I worked out the schedule for 900 students. That was before computers. We used cards with numbers on the edges and punched out the numbers corresponding to the courses selected. Then with a long spindle, we pulled out the class enrollments, a method that was time and labor intensive.

I had been working with about 60,000 of these cards all week and by Friday I was exhausted. I was scheduled to explain this new system at the Saturday faculty meeting. I remember sitting in front of the TV in community that Friday night, and one of the sisters said, "I'm going across the river"–meaning to get some booze (Oak Cliff was dry). I said, "Bring me some gin and tonic water." I'd never really had gin and tonic, but it sounded like a winner. All I remember was waking up in my bed, not knowing how I got there. Then the alarm went off and I got ready for the faculty meeting. I felt absolutely awful and the room was swimming around.

When I got to school Brother Adrian said, "Do you have that old back problem?" and I lied, "Yes;" whereupon he gave me a couple of his muscle, relaxant pills. I became extremely limp, and everything was still swimming. Coffee and donuts helped settle me down and I got through the meeting. It wasn't until the faculty party, at the end of that school year that I told Brother Adrian what had really happened.

To sum up these years, I'd say, "To question authority is to seek the truth."

CHAPTER 5

GOD BREAKS THROUGH INTO MY LIFE

God broke into my life at a stoplight in Oak Cliff, Dallas, in March 1970. Although God had spoken to me throughout my life, He broke into my life at that stoplight, setting in motion a series of events that would eventually affect many thousands of people.

I was a counselor at Bishop Dunne High School, but I lived at Saint James Convent and attended Mass at that parish. The pastor was immersed in starting a vibrant community of young people and adults called the *Happening*.

That community gathered for weekly Mass Saturday evenings at Saint James. I was impressed with their community spirit but, quite frankly, the hugging turned me off. It was 1969 and Vatican II's message of love had not penetrated my closed mind. I saw what seemed to be a genuine love in that community, and my heart began to melt.

The *Happening* seemed to come at me from all sides. Gail Smith, who helped me in the counseling office, was on the *Happening* team. Dan Luby, who taught at Bishop Dunne, was also on the *Happening* team. Then I invited a guest speaker, Mary Beth Orth, to speak to the seniors as part of their marriage course. She spoke frankly about being pregnant. After her talk I thanked her, and guess what! She told me about a wonderful new retreat for young people—the *Happening*.

Sister Patty Ridgley and I drove to school every day in my red beetle Volkswagen and she told me more about the *Happening*. God was breaking through my stubborn dislike of something that I really did not yet understand.

On Thursday afternoon, soon after Mary Beth's talk, I left my counseling office, I recall looking at the large, beautiful collage behind my desk. The collage had flowers of all kinds and the words, "All the flowers of all the tomorrows are in the seeds of today." I walked out into the sunshine and got into my red Volkswagen to drive home.

I stopped at a red light and from some place deep inside of me I heard the words, I am going to make the *Happening* tomorrow. The light changed to green in a matter of seconds and I sang my way home. I called Gail to see if there was room for me. There was.

That weekend I stepped out of my structured, rigid, predictable life devoid of most of the human race and entered the reality of human beings each of whom God loves infinitely and personally. The simple process of *the Happening* was: Who am I?... What is my relationship to others?... Who is God to me?... We listened to talks, not from experts and teachers, but from men, women and teenagers as they answered these three basic questions. I remember only two of the participants in my small group. One was a middle-aged man from Mexico. He could not read or write but knew the Bible and quoted whole chapters of it. He literally glowed when he spoke. The other person I remember was a young woman from the University of Dallas who was searching for a closer friendship with God.

Our group leaders were David (Mary Beth's husband) and Jerry. And then there was me. I was very emotional in answering the questions. I had never answered the basic question "Who am I?" On that *Happening* I tried to express the real me instead of talking about my roles. I was embarrassed and uncomfortable, but the people in my small group understood. Their acceptance of me gave me the courage to go on. Then I went on to talk about how I related to my father and mother, my sister and two brothers. In talking I discovered inside of me a mixture of feelings and a lot of judging.

On Saturday afternoon I listened to the Jesus talk and got in touch with my strong relationship with God. Those in my group shared their closeness to God. Everything got bigger and better through that personal sharing. I had never really focused that intently on such questions and certainly had never shared such intimate thoughts and feelings with anyone. That was a new and wonderful experience for me.

As we gradually encountered and revealed ourselves over the course of 44 hours, our lives were transformed. I left the *Happening* retreat feeling re-born. I had let go of the external symbols of my life that closed me off from others. I felt transparent. God spoke to me through this event and these real people. At the closing Mass, I, too, hugged and cried.

Little did I know then that, God, besides moving me to make the *Happening*, was also planting the seeds of what would become an essential part of the Beginning Experience process.

On Monday when I went back to Bishop Dunne High School, the world looked different, totally different. Each person was bright and beautiful. The *Happening* was a conversion experience for me. That was abundance.

I accepted the invitation to join the *Happening* team. Jo Lamia was already on the team. She was recently divorced and taught at St. Cecilia School. We became close friends.

In 1972, I changed jobs. I was still a Sister of Saint Mary and continued under my vow of obedience to my religious superiors when Father Bob Wilson asked my religious community for me to come, as a counselor, to work in Saint John's Parish in Fort Worth. (#14) He, too, was on the *Happening* team. At Saint John's, I lived in an experimental community near the church with three laywomen and two other sisters. We were learning that acceptance of one another was the foundation of peaceful living. We tried to live a real acceptance of differences by trying not to change each other.

Father Wilson drove me to the weekly *Happening* team meetings in Dallas. One evening on the way home he asked me to consider writing a weekend process for engaged couples. I said yes. God spoke again when I added, but only if Jo Lamia, (our divorced friend) would be involved with the engaged couples. She had something unique and powerful to say to those who were blindly in love and preparing to get married.

Jo and I attended the Marriage Encounter weekend so that I could write the Engaged Encounter. We were the odd couple, a divorced woman and a nun. We wrote on the Marriage Encounter questions and shared by reading our writing to each other, just the two of us in our small group.

Jo had never experienced writing of this kind and said. "Initially, I just did circles and push pulls like practicing for Palmer Method handwriting, until it began to flow–and when it did, it was a flood."

She discovered inside herself and through her writing, the answers to her long-asked and long-unanswered questions. She found out that the hiding of her feelings and her never being real to Peter, her former husband, was her part in the breakup of their marriage.

That realization really hit her hard. She cried and cried. I listened as she journeyed through her grief.

Before my eyes I saw the letting go and transformation of Jo from pain and confusion to new life. In the end she swept clean all the cobwebs, forgave herself and Peter, and closed the door gently but firmly on the past.

Although my conscious intent on that Marriage Encounter had been to write the Engaged Encounter, when I saw the healing Jo was experiencing, I began to see how a similar process of letting go could be used for the divorced and widowed people that I knew. **Here in Jo's journey I discovered the process of the Beginning Experience. This was not some text book invention; it was the profound discovery of the Beginning Experience process in Jo's journey from death to life. God was turning on floodlights of inspiration in me to write down that process.**

The Holy Spirit had inspired me when I stopped at the red light. That had been three years earlier. Then God had spoken again when I asked if Jo Lamia could be part of a retreat for engaged couples. But the biggest bang was the complete healing and letting go that Jo had experienced as she wrote and shared with me.

On that weekend she had bravely faced issues that she had not confronted before. At the end I saw a profound release, transformation, and new life in her. I saw Christ living His resurrected life in her. It was like a vision. I knew immediately that others could be transformed too.

We went on to create the Engaged Encounter and really had fun working with that first Engaged Encounter team. We did that for about two years, during which time I wrote the Beginning Experience process. I took Jo's Marriage Encounter journal and from her writing created the outlines for the Beginning Experience. Her writings were simple and direct. **I tried to distill a process that laid down layer upon layer a progression from self, to passing through grief, to trust, to facing guilt, to forgiving and being forgiven, to closing the door and finally to reaching out to others.** Jo and I looked at this simple outline and thought it contained all the phases of passing through grief to new life. (#s 15 and 16) But we needed to test it out with a Pilot Weekend.

God again broke through during that Pilot Weekend of Beginning Experience, October 18-20, 1974. When I lose sight of God's power and instead focus on my human limitations, I become immobilized by fear. That's what happened on the Pilot Weekend. I became physically ill from listening to all the pain in my own small group. I was not focused on the present here and now, and kept falling into fear of the future. How could these hurting people ever be trained and be ready in less than six weeks to become a team? I wanted to refund the participants $5 registration and send them all home. My insane fear would require a miraculous breakthrough from God.

The team took me to the altar and prayed for the Holy Spirit to come into me with God's strength and courage. As a result of that prayer from the community, I became willing to let go of my fear and continue with the weekend. It was thus that we finished the whole process and formed the first Beginning Experience team.

The Beginning Experience was birthed from the suffering, death and resurrection in Jo's life, in my life, and in the lives of those first participants. We learned that grief doesn't just go away. It must be gone through. We also learned that it is through the power of God breaking through each time that He heals each one on each weekend.

CHAPTER 6

THE PHENOMENAL GROWTH OF THE BEGINNING EXPERIENCE

God broke into my life with the miraculous gift of Beginning Experience. God continued to nurture this fledgling ministry in unplanned and unexpected ways. Sometimes God was working against my fears.

I have always had a very hard time letting go and letting God. So in God's infinite wisdom the Holy Spirit took my control away by making me stone deaf right after the October Pilot weekend. I couldn't hear any of the talks in preparation for the real weekend in December. It was to be presented by brand new team members from the Pilot, and I thought they needed a lot of teaching and direction. Because of my total deafness, which lasted a few months, I was rendered powerless to guide this fledgling team. So Jo Lamia gracefully stepped up, providing the guidance needed to form the team for the December weekend. She always let go and let God.

Starting with that first December weekend, this new team went on to present brilliant and effective weekends while I was learning to let go and let the Holy Spirit work. Each weekend was full to overflowing. I was learning that God works very well through unfinished, imperfect and hesitant people. **I was beginning to live the process of Beginning Experience which is the slow and difficult journey from control to letting go.**

Judith Tate had come to that first December weekend. She subsequently wrote a glowing article for *Agape Magazine*. As a result of this publicity, I was deluged with a wave of requests to bring the program to various states. Even though I was still working full time at Saint John's, I attempted to answer each letter with no secretary or staff.

In response to one request that came from Pittsburgh, a group of men and women from our team flew to Pittsburgh and presented the weekend, resulting in an immediate success. However, this venture was another red light for me. It showed me that we needed much more than just "doing the weekend." We needed a manual, training and planned expansion. The Pittsburgh Beginning Experience floundered and eventually discontinued. That painful experience pushed me to start thinking about writing a manual.

Providentially, I had taped all of the talks during the weekends of that first year. In a real sense these taped talks became the essence of *The Manual for Beginning Experience*. The first thing I did toward writing *The Manual* was to listen to all the talks. I danced around the living room for sheer joy in re-experiencing each one's story. I was in a sort of ecstasy at the power of God. It was clear to me that the Holy Spirit had transformed these men and women into resurrected people.

Then I listened carefully to each talk and wrote detailed outlines. Thus it was that that brand new Dallas/Fort Worth team wrote *The Manual*. I was the scribe. I felt pushed, driven, almost obsessed to write it all down. Then I was pulled back to earth with the task of getting it typed. That was before computers. I found a wonderful volunteer who took my handwritten pages and typed them.

The Paulist Center in Boston hosted the first ever meeting of separated and divorced Catholics from all over the United States. Jo Lamia and I planned to attend.

Jerry and Suzanne Jeansonne from the Pilot weekend had married and moved to Boston. I asked them if Jo and I could come and live with them for two weeks in order to write *The Manual*. I had no file cabinet. I put the typed pages and rough draft for *The Manual* in a lovely picnic basket. So with my picnic basket, we got ready to board the plane to Boston. I cautiously watched as that picnic basket went out of sight through the X-ray machine. It came out all in one piece. So we boarded the plane and put the picnic basket above us in the storage bin. We were on our way to the Paulist Center in Boston.

Three memories stand out for me about the Paulist meeting. First, we did an impromptu workshop in an overcrowded room. Thus, many more people heard of the Beginning Experience. Second, one person, Mary Lou Murphy of Seattle, literally attached herself to me everywhere I went, sweetly demanding that we come and start the Beginning Experience in Seattle. Third, the North American Conference of Separated and Divorced Catholics (NACSDC) was formed.

After the conference, Jo and I worked diligently for two weeks with Suzanne as editor and typist, and Jerry as evaluator. The finished pages went back into the picnic basket and we came home. My task then was to transform these pages into field copies to meet the growing demand for starting new teams. During that time we identified central points for clusters of cities that had requested the Beginning Experience.

The first such "cluster" was centered in Davenport, Iowa, in March 1976. A team of six went to Davenport. We had participants coming from Kansas City; Columbus, Ohio; Grand Rapids, Michigan; Minneapolis; Seattle (yes, Mary Lou); Boston; and Alaska. All arrived on the designated Friday, promptly by 7:00 p.m. at St. Ambrose College and Seminary, prepared to start. But we were locked out of our building. I prayed to let go and let God, and to take it easy. Since we couldn't start until the next morning we spent Friday evening visiting and getting acquainted. The big comedy was that the men were uncomfortably housed in an old unused building. One man actually checked into a nearby motel.

We made the best of that bump in the road. That night we located the key, rearranged the Friday evening schedule to fit into Saturday morning, laughed a lot, and put ourselves in God's hands. Our presentation room was a classroom surrounded by the seminary Saturday classes. The women were housed in a dorm next to the bedrooms of the seminarians. That was a unique situation–the first of many "unique situations." The marvel of the process and the flexibility of these new team members produced a very successful weekend. Six new teams were formed as a result of the weekend and the training on Monday.

We had no manual. We only had the field copies which we were testing and only cartoon transparencies, which eventually became the training slide show. Actually presenting that weekend before publishing *The Manual* and training materials was an excellent way of finding the mistakes and making necessary additions. One such important addition was suggested by the priest who came from Grand Rapids. He noted that we needed to have a structured way of saying goodbye to the weekend itself so that no one would leave unprepared for the rude awakening of going home.

In our early history we had gotten a request from Air Force chaplain Father Marcantonio in Colorado Springs. A group from our "just formed" Dallas/ Fort Worth team went in October 1975 to present the weekend there. God's big surprise was that at the "Rite of Reconciliation," Father Marc knelt down and said "Before you confess your sins, I am asking you to forgive the Church because I am aware that some in the Church have shut the door on you. I invite you to come to me and forgive the Church." Each one went up to him and touched him saying "I forgive you for—." **Father Marc had a profound understanding of the essence of forgiveness: letting go and forgiving another opens the door for God's grace to enter in. Forgiving the Church was needed before confessing one's sins. Because it was "of the essence" of forgiveness, this ceremony became thereafter an important part of "Reconciliation.** Then this wonderful man, Father Marc, was transferred to Anchorage, Alaska, where he started Beginning Experience.

By mid-year 1976, we had teams functioning in Kansas City, Columbus, Grand Rapids, Minneapolis, Boston, Colorado Springs and Oklahoma City. All because of the inspiration of the Holy Spirit, lots of hard work, and people moving from one place to another!

The cluster-training idea really worked. Another cluster-training took place in Saint Paul in February 1977. Minnesota in February is frozen solid. I had never before seen a frozen lake. I was blown away. I looked out my bedroom window and saw a big heavy truck driving on the frozen water of Lake Rogers. That unusual sight gave me a symbol for the redemptive power of the Beginning Experience prevailing over unresolved frozen grief.

Father Guy Gau, Family Life Director from South Dakota attended. He was particularly impressed and wanted to begin the program. All the participants were ready to go back home and start the Beginning Experience. Teams from that cluster were started in South Dakota and North Dakota, Chicago and several locations in Minnesota and Iowa. We were expanding rapidly. It seemed to me that God had let loose a run-away-horse and I was trying to keep up.

From the beginning, I tried to establish communication among our new teams. We distributed a Newsletter, written by a talented and energetic volunteer editor, Jody Galier. She eventually quit her job with an oil company and became my assistant. Here's the story.

In order to educate our diocesan parish ministers in 1976 about the grief of divorced people, our team members presented a panel in which they told their personal stories of how the Beginning Experience had brought them through the grief process from death to new life. After that moving presentation, I indicated that I was hoping to be able to employ an assistant. Sister Mary Dorothy, director of the Fort Worth diocesan office, came up to me and told me that her aunt had died and had left her $14,000. Now that she knew of our need and the value of this ministry, she would petition our Sisters of Saint Mary administration to give that money to the Beginning Experience; it was the exact amount of money that I had told Jody we would pay her. At the time I had no idea where the money would come from. I believe that God miraculously provided the money, down to the last penny.

I dreamed of having a gathering of all the teams in 1977. Father Marc offered to host the western half of the United States in Colorado Springs and the Columbus, Ohio team hosted the Eastern half of the United States. So the "13 original" teams met. We prayed, worked, laughed, cried, danced and created family. The highlight for me was July 7, 1977 (7-7-77) standing in a circle at Pikes Peak for Mass and then singing "Go Now in Peace."

I began dreaming even more passionately of a national gathering. At the end of the Colorado and Columbus events we were unified because the use of *The Manual* and the new *Training Slide Presentation* put the "13 Originals" on the same page. Group energy was sky-rocketing and all-embracing. We had the momentum to plan a National Convention.

The following year we gathered in Chicago. Many men and women from each team came for the land-mark event–our first National Convention in 1978! Each team made its own banner right there and we had a lively "Parade of Teams." I was enthralled.

That afternoon, as we were making the last minute preparations, I suddenly had an "out of body experience." I was lifted up above all the people and had a breathtaking "bird's eye view" of Beginning Experience. Then I was softly lowered. The vision has stayed with me always, providing me hope in the face of difficulties. My vision also signaled to me that the National Convention would have far reaching implications for the ministry. The keynote address was of great significance. My professor from Southern Methodist University, Dr. Harville Hendrix, gave it. He enthusiastically confirmed the value of the Beginning Experience. He also warned us to avoid sentimentality which can be a counterfeit of real grieving.

Judith Tate and the Oklahoma City team presented the first ever book published about the journey of people through the Beginning Experience process. The title, *Learning to Live Again, The Journey Through Grief for the Widowed or Divorced,* captured the essence of the stories of the people of the Beginning Experience.

As a body–as an assembly–we decided to have a nine-member national board. Nominations were gathered from those at the convention and the first board meeting was set for January 1979. We were moving quickly and surely under the guidance of the Holy Spirit.

I had mixed feelings about the new board. Part of me was very glad to be turning all this responsibility over to a group of people. Another part was very afraid of letting go. I was making a significant choice of putting all decisions in those new hands and hearts. I could have chosen to have a consultative or advisory board. I had watched other organizations flounder under the weight of the founder's scrutiny and control. I chose to make that new board a decision-making board, to give them all the responsibility. **My decision was a profound letting go which led to abundance of life for this ministry.**

The Board Meeting set the tone and foundation for the future of the ministry. It contained well designed guidelines for expansion and accountability. It was like a family reunion with home cooking. I made my famous vegetable soup and delicious slow baked brisket, which all devoured. Gene O'Brien, board member from Oklahoma City, proposed marriage to our secretary, Judith Tate.

It was memorable too because the Board decided to present a cluster weekend and training in Honolulu for Hawaii, New Zealand and Australia. That expansion was to be our first venture outside the United States.

CHAPTER 7

ANOTHER WORLD AWAY

Hawaii, Australia, New Zealand

What had begun as a local program was fast becoming global. Taking the Beginning Experience to the South Pacific changed both the direction of this ministry and of my life.

I had been corresponding (no e-mail yet) with a priest from Sydney, Australia. He had heard of Beginning Experience at Notre Dame University in a course on reaching out to divorced people. Then, almost simultaneously, the "Solo Parents" in New Zealand wrote asking to start Beginning Experience there. At that same time, a woman from Honolulu contacted me. My geographic wheels started turning. What about doing a cluster in Hawaii with Australians and New Zealanders coming?

Jody, by now, had started as my assistant. She and I organized that complicated correspondence with the Hawaiians, Australians and New Zealanders. We also gathered a training team from California, Boston, South Dakota, Houston and Dallas/Fort Worth. I made sure that all the talks were covered and since the talks had not been assigned to individuals, I asked each presenter to bring all their talks.

At first, I did not intend to go. I was trying to let go and let others do that exciting venture. But deep down I really wanted to go. I'm not sure when I changed my mind, but thank God I did.

The agreement that I made with Hawaii and the training team members was simple. Hawaii would provide the housing and food for two weeks and procure a venue for the weekend. The training team members would pay their own air fare. We coordinated arrivals at the Honolulu airport. What Jo Lamia did not know was that Sharon, her dear friend who had moved to California, was coming. That had been my little secret.

We arrived at the airport within an hour of each other. We were "collected" with all our luggage in an old red pickup. It took several trips to get us to our new home. Still there was no sign of Sharon.

I was really "sweating it" fearing that all of us would be taken and Sharon would be left. Suddenly Jo said, "Look there is someone on the other side of the glass that looks just like Sharon." Indeed it was. Their hug was huge and tears flowed.

We stayed in a high school dorm building with the men on one floor, the women on another and the community area for meals and meetings on another. We arrived on Wednesday which would have given us plenty of time to prepare for the weekend. Since none of us had worked together and none of the talks had been assigned, I firmly believed it was imperative that on Thursday we would coordinate and review the talks, and that we would all get on the same page.

However soon after we arrived, everyone walked down to the nearest beach and played. I was intending to have a "big meeting" to put everything together. After all, we had people from Australia and New Zealand traveling and spending their money to make the weekend and take it home, and we didn't even know who was doing what.

So at breakfast Thursday, I suggested that we spend the morning putting the weekend together. There was unified mutiny and every-one left for the beach. After all we were in Hawaii.

Earlier that morning, I had awakened to the marvelous sound of tropical birds singing and the gurgling of a waterfall. I was in para-dise. I had given the day to God and prayed that the Holy Spirit would guide us in "getting it all together." A better prayer would have been for the gift of acceptance and of letting go and letting God.

I tried to relax and play on the beach and in the waves, but my insides were churning. My anxiety level had sky-rocketed. The Australians and New Zealanders arrived and they too went to the beach.

It wasn't until early Friday afternoon, the day of the start of the weekend, that we all went out to the venue and had the "big meet-ing." It all fell into place. God was the power that brought it together. I had been forced to let go and let God.

We had no presentation room and so we improvised by using the stairs. The presenters sat at the top of the stairs and the participants sat on the stairs below. This worked.

Actually, absolutely everything worked out well. I was just now beginning to trust the process that God had given to Jo and me. My fear was that we would fail if I didn't supervise every detail of that important weekend. With my controlling nature, I had to know that all the talks were good and that each team person knew exactly what to do ahead of time. But all of the men and women on the presenting team had received excellent training at home. They knew that and believed that playing on the beach in Hawaii was more important than obeying my fear and compulsion.

If Beginning Experience could survive the Hawaii experience and my fears, it could survive anything. The success of that venture demonstrated that having *The Manual* and unified training throughout the United States could guarantee the integrity of the program. In addition, the participants in Hawaii were genuine in seeking healing, and their attitude assured success.

Every waking moment after the Beginning Experience weekend, we played on the beaches. Then the following weekend we conducted the intensive training so that those little groups could go home and present their Pilot Weekends. Teams would start in Honolulu, Hawaii; Christchurch, New Zealand; and Sydney, Australia.

Father Guy did an excellent job of training. I observed his understanding and love for the process and his expertise in teaching. So I began to think about stepping aside and having him take over as the next Director to guide the Beginning Experience through its next phase. I often joked that I'd found Father Guy on the beach in Hawaii.

During the "play week" after the weekend, Eddie, who was the awesome photographer, took me to the Ala Moana shopping center where I found and fell in love with the pink/rose/purple/sunrise/sunset fabric which became my hallmark garment–my famous "pink mumu." Much later Father Guy questioned, "Josephine, don't you have another dress to wear?" I said "Yes, but this is my favorite and I hope to be buried in it." He quipped, "I don't know anyone else who goes around wearing their shroud."

From August to November we planned for Jo Lamia and me to go for the Pilot Weekends in Australia and New Zealand. That was taking Beginning Experience to far away places.

We arrived in Sydney in early November 1979, and although we wanted to go to bed early, we took the advice of the Aussies and stayed up until 10:00 p.m., advice that worked well. Our bodies never suffered jet lag, and we were able to enjoy the next day and the whole time there.

On the plane descending into Sydney, little girls passed out "lollies"–caramels. I said, "Jo, do you have a hard center in yours?" She said, "No." The hard center in my caramel was the gold crown of my tooth. I saved it. On the second day in Sydney, I went to a dentist with the crown in hand. He cemented it in place. It's still secure.

The venue for the Pilot Weekend was great: large presentation room, lovely chapel and nice small group rooms. It was the Hilton compared to Hawaii's stairwell. The location was a distance from Sydney in the "bush" or forest area. On Saturday night, after the last presentation, when all were supposed to be in bed, I heard loud and raucous laughing on the parking lot. The National Board had tried so hard to tell teams in the United States to stop having team parties on Saturday night, when everyone was supposed to be in bed. So, my mind was racing. "How could this forbidden custom have gotten across the Pacific Ocean to Australia?" "Was it a devious form of the universal subconscious that C.G. Jung spoke about?" So off I went to the parking lot to remedy that situation. All I found were lots of birds. The next day I learned that Kukabara birds sound exactly like laughing human beings. So these birds were the forbidden Saturday night party.

The Aussies did a superb job of conducting their Pilot Weekend. Their presentations were very personal and true to the process. A week later we conducted an intensive training for those participants who wanted to form the new team. The Beginning Experience of Sydney was established. Their initial team had fine and professional people who carried the torch.

Jo and I flew to Christchurch, New Zealand. The "Solo Parent" women there embraced us with their hospitality and abundance. Even though they were poor materially, they were rich in spirit. We visited several support groups and were absolutely amazed at these groups where the women actually physically, financially and emotionally supported one another in every way. They had formed real community.

The American holiday of Thanksgiving fell on the day before their Pilot Weekend. Shirley and Judith, two New Zealanders who had been trained in Hawaii, took us on a day-long outing over the hills to

Akaroa, an international port and fishing village. It was getting to be 6:00 p.m. and we were still in Akaroa. The turkey had not been put into the oven and thirty guests were arriving at Shirley's at 7:30 for Thanksgiving dinner with the Americans. Jo was nervous and kept asking me, "Do they know how long a turkey takes?" We stopped and bought a garbage bag full of lobster claws and headed home. The turkey was put into the oven. I had never heard of a "convection" oven, but that's what it was. While the turkey was cooking they boiled the lobster claws and cracked and peeled them, making lobster cocktails. The guests arrived at 7:30 with their electric skillets containing roasted vegetables, potatoes and pumpkin. We had a leisurely time sipping a delicious liqueur, then eating the lobster cocktails. Around 8:00 the turkey was done and the veggies were perfect. We sat down for a memorable New Zealand Thanksgiving feast. It was topped off, not with pumpkin pie (the pumpkin had been fried and served as a vegetable), but with pavlova, a meringue dessert fit for royalty.

The Pilot Weekend started the next day. The venue was an old home located up on top of a hill, accessible only on foot. So with the help of two teenage boys, we (four Christchurch team women, Jo and I) carried all the supplies, including the mattresses, up the hill to Saint Evelyn's retreat. New Zealand is very hilly and everyone walks and carries. After all the gear was carried up the hill and put in place, Jo and I were left alone while the others made another trip into town. Jo realized that she had left one of her talks at Shirley's where we were staying. So I picked up the phone to call Shirley, but the phone was backwards, numbering from 9 to 1. I tried dialing her, but to no avail. So I dialed "O" and told the operator that the phone was backwards and I couldn't get the number. The voice on the other end said, "You bloody Yanks, it's supposed to be backwards here in New Zealand," and then she connected me to Shirley.

In the meantime, we put the mattresses on the beds, got things ready and had time to take in the gorgeous scenery. Our room looked out over the sparkling Pacific Ocean and down the hill covered with cascades of daisies and pink roses. That view has become my "place of peace" in my meditations.

The New Zealanders' talks were from the heart, reflecting their pain and joy. They had prepared completely. (#s 17 and 18) The Saturday night entertainment was hysterically funny. The New Zealanders made Jo eat a vegemite (the famous Vitamin B rich, pungent, dark brown spread) sandwich.

A priest in Jo's small group who had been sent by his bishop to "check out" this new program, hugged me and Jo on Sunday morning and said, "You made me love you." I suspected that he would reflect that in his report to the bishop.

A week later we conducted the intensive training for those participants who became the first New Zealand Beginning Experience team. Jo and I left convinced that the new team was established on a firm foundation.

The experience of New Zealand was a real turning point in my life. I didn't want to ever lose the simple wonder of it all. I had seen joyful abundance in the simple lives of the "solo parents." Although they had very little, they shared generously and easily with one another. They cared for each other as family. They lived happily a simple life-style, devoid of surplus and clutter. They lived in the midst of unspeakable natural beauty.

As Jo and I left the Christchurch air terminal, walking to climb into our small plane that would take us to Auckland and our international flight home, I cried so hard that I thought I would become ill. My gut-wrenching anguish was muffled by the roar of the plane. As I cried, I vowed to return to New Zealand for a year to live with these wonderful people. I dreamed of capturing their way of life and their values and bringing these back in me.

The gift that the Solo Parents in New Zealand gave to us during the short two weeks that we lived with them far outweighed our gift of Beginning Experience to them. I never hesitated in my determination to spend at least a year being with them learning first-hand from them.

CHAPTER 8

MY SABBATICAL IN NEW ZEALAND

My First Three Months

The Beginning Experience had been the main reason I went to New Zealand in the first place. It was there that I experienced another way of looking at life and the world. It was there, as I boarded the plane home, that I vowed to go back for a year. I began immediately to lay the groundwork.

First of all, I prepared by boldly asking the New Zealand Beginning Experience team people, to give me room and board. I hoped to live with different families and to work for them in whatever way they needed. Secondly, I wrote to the New Zealand Consul General in Los Angeles assuring him that, while in New Zealand, I would not be working to earn money or take a job from a New Zealander. Thirdly, I arranged with my religious community, the Sisters of Saint Mary, for a sabbatical year. The Sisters did not hesitate to provide for me during that year. I felt proud and grateful for my generous community. I was the first Sister, in our province to arrange for a sabbatical, and thus paved the way for others to do the same.

But still, I had to come up with the airfare. I had been spending a day a week relaxing and painting in the art loft of our motherhouse. So when confronted with the cost of the plane ticket to this faraway place, I decided to paint my way there. I literally mass-produced little "outhouse" paintings. I painted the skies on thirty five canvasses, then the outhouses, the grass, the fences, the Sears catalogs and all the finishing touches of flowers and birds. Many of my friends still have these outhouses in their bathrooms. I sold them all, plus most of my other paintings. It was a fun way to get my ticket.

I went back to New Zealand after Father Guy was securely in place as the new Executive Director. My intention was to be in New Zealand for my fiftieth birthday, which was October 12, 1981. So all was arranged for my trip. God arranged lots of synchronicity to surprise me for this great adventure. On September 21, 1981, I flew from Los Angeles to New Zealand.

In Christchurch, I heard many stories and tried to translate the New Zealand expressions into my American brain. I spent the day before my birthday at the Crown Court Number 2, hearing the case of the twelve anti-Springbok protesters who had broken into and occupied the Rugby Union Headquarters in Christchurch. They were arrested for protesting that the rugby Springbok team from South Africa had no blacks on it. South Africa was coming to play a very important series of rugby games in New Zealand.

Seven of the protesters presented their own defense and five others were represented by an attorney. The expert witnesses included two professors from the University of Canterbury who were from South Africa and had trained the protesters in non-violent methods. That event was my first experience of non-violent protest. The crowded courtroom was electric.

In view of all that had transpired in South Africa, that event for me was impressive. I had only read about Apartheid and the cruel imprisonment of Nelson Mandela. (At this point, he would remain in prison for 14 more years.) I was moved to attend the entire court session. The protesters defended themselves in compelling ways. They had used every method to make another voice in New Zealand heard and to say to the world that racism must stop. That first week in New Zealand was a bright light focused on the heart of the New Zealand people. Justice is in their blood.

On my birthday, I met Shirley down at the statue of Queen Victoria in the square. It was the first time I caught the bus there. When I asked for Victoria Station the driver shouted, "You're not in bloody England, lady!" I made a lot of mistakes, laughable ones.

Shirley and I went to the Botanic Gardens. It was sheer delight to see these gardens. It was full Spring in the Southern Hemisphere.

Afterwards Shirley and I went to the sentencing of the twelve convicted protesters. Although the defendants' pleas had been very moving, in the end, they were all convicted and fined. Later we joined the group of protesters at the Oxford Inn Pub where they all toasted me for my birthday and cheered, "Hip, Hip, Hooray!" At the end of those two days, I had a positive view of non-violent protesting. I saw how many New Zealanders were serious about letting their native people–the Maori–and the Blacks of South Africa–know that they had a voice.

What I witnessed in this trial was significant for me. On that birthday I decided to work for peace.

In January, I accompanied my friend, Judith, who was planning a move to Wellington. We went by train from Christchurch to Picton, and by ferry to Wellington. On the train trip north from Christchurch through Kaikoura, we saw velvet green hills, sheep and lambs scampering away at the sound of the train, the rugged Pacific Ocean crashing on the volcanic rock shore and the snow covered mountains in the distance to the left.

The ferry crossing from Picton to Wellington took us through a narrow channel. Then we went out into Cook Strait, very treacherous water between the North Island and the South Island, and into a foggy Wellington harbor. We passed huge rocks which had caused many shipwrecks.

While in Wellington, I attended a Zamfir Concert. Zamfir is a beloved native of Rumania. He played the pan flute beautifully, accompanied by a sprightly little old man, dressed in folk attire. I was transported into another world by that performance. After the concert I went back stage to meet them. I wound up translating his French into English for the bystanders. I purchased several of his tapes and, later frequently just sat for hours listening to his soothing music. Thus Zamfir was a constant companion for my year in New Zealand.

For the first few weeks, I lived in Christchurch with Judith. The young woman who lived "over the road" (across the street) taught me how to spin. She was in the last month of her pregnancy and I invited myself over to use her wheel. I had gotten a beautiful white fleece at Show Day. During the next few weeks, I spun six skeins of wool. Spinning is a slow relaxing process. The raw wool, filled with lanolin, had such a good feel on my skin. My hands became soft and smooth. I didn't have any deadlines or projects in New Zealand. I was truly living one moment at a time. Spinning became a symbol of the freedom I was living.

From Christchurch, I went to spend three months on the North Island on the Coromandel Peninsula. I lived with John and Anne Brier who owned and worked a sheep farm. They had invited "this

American lady" to come and stay with them and to experience a real aspect of New Zealand life.

Prior to going to the Coromandel, I went to a native Maori funeral with the priest who had been at the deathbed of an elderly Maori man and so the priest was part of the funeral or *Tangi*. He invited me to accompany him. I didn't want to intrude with my white skin, but when I got inside I felt totally accepted. There were welcoming speeches each time a Maori family arrived. The elders welcomed them and then sang the entire genealogy of each family. One at a time people approached the body, which was laid out on a jade slab and was covered with gauze lace and flowers, and spoke directly to him. They said everything in their hearts: the good things, the bad things, all the unfinished business and their goodbyes. The Maori people believe that the person's soul is still in the body until it is put in the ground. What a simple, meaningful closure for each one!

Every Maori related to the deceased comes, is almost required to come, to the *Tangi*. This means that at the time of each funeral the freezing works of New Zealand (where export lamb is processed) come to a screeching halt.

After all the goodbyes, we went into the dining area and feasted on lobster and all kinds of goodies and celebrated the deceased's life. During these festivities I talked to Martin Solomon who had big, big hair. He was a lobster fisherman from Kaikoura (which means lobster). He explained the *Tangi* and he invited me to come and stay with him and his family and to go lobster fishing with him.

My Time on the Coromandel

Coromandel is the rugged peninsula where New Zealanders go to vacation. I flew from Christchurch to Auckland on the North Island. A friend drove me to Anne and John Brier's. At the highest point we could see the Hauraki Gulf, the city of Auckland, all of the Coromandel Peninsula and the vast Pacific Ocean to the east.

The first moments in the Brier's home seemed awkward: with five children, Kelly, Gerard, Brandon, Daniel and Robert, plus the news that I'd have to stay in the house with the family and all five kids, for a week or two, because the sheep shearers were in the batch (cabin) intended for me. In addition, their cousins were coming the day after the shearers. I had previously told my friend who drove me that I intended to be on my own, living in their batch and would not get involved with the Briers. What a laugh! That just tells you how unreal, controlling and self-centered I was.

After I arrived, we all went off to Saturday evening Mass at the tiny church in Coromandel town. Father Theo presided over the simple, prayerful liturgy. The Briers seemed to be the youngest family there. During Mass, Father Theo's dog lay under the altar and, after communion, Father Theo held little Robert, the Brier's baby, who played with the priest's beard. After Mass, I met three people who would be important in my life in the Coromandel: Mabs, Joe and Dr. Arey.

Monday was shearing day for the Briers. John was at the wool shed at 6:00 a.m. Anne was charged with preparing a big breakfast at the house for 7:30 a.m. as well as a big lunch and morning and afternoon tea. Her part in the shearing was vital and a lot of work. I went down with her to take morning tea and stayed. Both boys, Brandon and Daniel, were in the shed all day. I learned that they stay with their dad most of the time, while he does all the chores around the farm. Anne and John are partners in the ownership of the farm and in all the work and decisions.

There were three shearers and a sweeper. Keith was the lead shearer, having broken a world record in shearing eight hundred sheep in a nine-hour day. All the workers were fast and skillful. The Maori sweeper had a tough time keeping up with them. She swept the dirty bum wool to one side, and then swept and separated the middle grade belly wool, from the best back wool. I was assigned to weigh the wool that came from the ewes that had given birth to twins. The twinning ewes had a notch cut on the ear so I knew which wool to retrieve and then weigh.

John and the boys baled the wool by stomping it down in a baler. The wool was then compressed into jute bales marked with the name of the farm and numbered. Fifteen hundred sheep were shorn that day yielding 32 bales, each selling for about $600, representing about half of the annual income of the farm.

At noon sharp, all the workers went to the house for lunch which lasted for one hour exactly. Then they continued the shearing until about 2:30 at which time the shearers and the sweeper all sat on the floor and drank beer–two flagons each–and ate sandwiches before leaving to go to town.

The shearers were a marvel to watch, never wasting a motion. (A) In addition to baling the wool, John worked the sheep dogs so that there were always sheep ready in the pens. It was a simple, primitive, almost ageless operation. There was much hard work to be done and done well, and finished without a lot of fuss and fanfare. This is the quality of the New Zealanders that I learned to appreciate.

Shearing is a filthy job. We came home and I took a shower. Wool, full of lanolin and shit, is dirty and I had really gotten into it, weighing those fleeces. I had a certain sense of triumph in that shower, congratulating myself that I had been a real part of sheep shearing. The Brier's farm (or some people would call it a sheep station) was three thousand acres of fairly mountainous terrain. The whole farm is divided into paddocks separated from each other by thick hedges. From a hill it looked like a green patchwork quilt. All of the paddocks had to be planted with grass seed and fertilized. A little top dressing plane flew back and forth over the mountainous area, spreading the seed and fertilizer. The plane took off from the highest point of the farm. That summit is where I went on Holy Thursday, to paint my first-ever spontaneous watercolor of the Hauraki Gulf. Until that point I had been painting in oils.

My batch was like a little motel unit with the shower and toilet attached to the porch. There were six-foot tall blooming hydrangeas next to the porch. Inside were two rooms: a kitchen and a bedroom. The first night, the friendly bull was just outside my window, literally shaking the batch. I was petrified. I couldn't go outside to use the restroom. I stayed in bed all night in fear. Next day, Anne and John laughed about this bull which was loose on the property.

The Brier children were very different from one another. Kelly, eight years old, was the only girl. She was red headed and freckled faced. She commanded respect. She was a leader. Right after I arrived, she took me to see the pigs and got right into the pen with them. She was fearless. Gerard was seven and a bit shy. He knew everything about running the farm because he worked with John. I helped him with his reading and he often came along and sketched beside me. Brandon was five. He was a charmer, darling looking, like an Irish lad.

I was very close to Daniel who was two. (#19) He always wore gum boots (heavy rubber boots for the mud). Between my batch and the house was a little creek with a bridge. In the morning I'd hear Daniel stomping across that bridge. Instead of saying "Good morning, Josephine," he'd say, "Dophine, go 'way." This lasted for a few days. Then he became my good friend. He spent most of his time mustering the sheep on the motorcycle with his dad. Daniel would sit between John's legs on the seat. The sheepdogs rode in a cart in back. Daniel had learned to call the sheep dogs. Crossing one leg in front of the other, putting his hand on his hip, Daniel called the dogs exactly like his dad.

Robert was nine months old, in diapers and crawling around the kitchen and living area. I was nervous with him crawling everywhere. I helped care for him by washing his diapers and then bleaching them on the grass like I had done in Belgium. Robert managed to hold his own as the youngest in the family.

Once I got settled into the batch, I spent some weekends with Mabs. She had lived for 30 years in South Africa. When World War II broke out in 1941, she had enlisted in the South African army as a nurse. Much later she met and married a South African doctor who died ten years later. Then she had returned to her native New Zealand and, eventually, married Frank. He had died a year before I met her. She was a delightful "English" lady. We became friends and shared our common interest in art. She and I attended the university art classes at the high school.

Another friend of the Briers was Joe O'Neil, a wonderful man who had been in prison for four years for being a conscientious objector in World War II. He was a real theologian. He had a beautiful Japanese garden in which he placed the Stations of the Cross that were made by Dr. Arey. Joe had been a librarian in Auckland most of his life after prison. He was a hard worker, having cleared all the gorse from his land before building his house. He had a lovely collection of art in his home.

Mabs and I attended a wonderful art weekend at the home of Barry Brickle. The rest of the group were local artists and others from Australia and China who knew of the famous New Zealand potter. He had constructed a home with lots of nooks and crannies for us to spread out in and to sketch. I sketched a great pot with the rain dripping down on it. When I started I didn't have a clue about how to draw it. The art teacher from Thames came by and gave me a few pertinent clues about drawing cylinders and I got "stuck into it" and really enjoyed shading in the darks until I finished a good drawing. (B) My confidence was boosted. This experience got me started in sketching and from then on I sketched everything I could, all over New Zealand.

That evening Mabs invited Joe for tea. We had a lovely curry sauce and scallops from "over the road," in the Hauraki Gulf. Next day Mabs and I went for another day of sketching. We went up on the narrow gauge railway, deep into the bush, over sideless bridges, past much native forest and Ponga (fern trees). I did a charcoal sketch of the bush and a pile of pine logs. Then I tried India ink and a watercolor wash of the Ponga.

I didn't like either of them as much as my big pot done the day before. We returned by the narrow gauge railway and displayed all our work for Barry and for a reporter from the Coromandel newspaper. We each gave two pictures for the library exhibit.

Mabs and I went to the Kauri Walk where I sketched the Kauri until it started raining. (C) The Kauri are huge trees that were found all over the peninsula. The hard wood was once used for ship building. One of the Kauri trees in the bush is reckoned to be 2,000 years old. Unfortunately, the bush was felled and burned by the early settlers and much of the native timber was never replaced, so the few native bush areas are very precious. I loved just sitting near the trail sketching these magnificent Kauri–an experience of peace and eternity among those ancient trees.

Mabs taught me to sketch in ink, not pencil, which can be erased and re-done to gain "perfection." The temptation to perfection can be the downfall of an artist. The first little ink sketch that I did was a pot of daisies on her breakfast table. (D) I just sketched it quickly and from then on I saw and recorded the world through ink. **Sketching in ink became for me a discipline of letting go and then being surprised at the wonder flowing from my pen. That was abundance– unplanned, spontaneous abundance.**

Mabs connected me to other interesting people. I sensed that the Coromandel "collects" a wonderful assortment of talented, educated and artistic people, one of which was Dr. Arey.

For twenty years, Dr. Arey had been the only doctor on the Coromandel Peninsula. She established the hospital in order to give her personal patient care there. She told me that when she was eight years old, back in England, she decided to be a country doctor. In medical school she decided on Coromandel, New Zealand. She had become a vital part of the whole peninsula. She was a strict Roman Catholic convert. She had sculpted the Stations of the Cross in the little church. Although she never read newspapers or magazines, she had a huge theological library and, like Joe O'Neil was a theologian.

She invited me to accompany her as she drove up and down the peninsula visiting people. She prepared a picnic basket and met me at Mass. We drove up the West coast and stopped for morning tea at a spot in view of two long waterfalls. At lunch we sat in the tall, soft grass under a Pahutukawa tree. Its gnarled roots hugged the rocky shoreline and extended into the water. The Pahutukawa trees have brilliant scarlet cluster blooms at Christmas.

We stopped at Colville and met a woman whose family had come twenty years earlier from Pennsylvania just after the Three-Mile-Island nuclear spill. They came as far away from Pennsylvania as they could. The family had occupied a farm at the tiptop of the Coromandel. Their sons and daughters lived in various houses overlooking a secluded bay.

Each view of the journey along the west coast was spectacular! It rained part of the time and was sunshiny part of the time and was nearly always windy.

Dr. Arey had built a tiny log batch at Kennedy's Bay and Father Theo had decided to use it for his desert retreats. She feared that new people would come to Coromandel and change it. Many feared that Father Theo would draw too many people for his desert retreats and, also, that artists and writers from overseas would come. The tension was, on the one hand, how to welcome people who came to create, to be renewed, and to live; and on the other hand, how to maintain the unique character of the Coromandel. And then there was the fear that the Saudi's and Iranian's would purchase thousands of acres of land. That dilemma was very real.

I rejoiced that I had seen a spot on earth of such beauty! The natural world and people emitted God's energy. I meditated on the Kauri and the Ponga giving off creative energy for thousands of years. At that time, I was reading Meister Eckhart who wrote about creation giving off divine energy. I thanked God for my experience of the sea, the mountains, the native bush, the sunsets, the Pahutukawa, the Ponga, the flowers, the six- foot tall hydrangeas, the sheep, the people, the greens, the blues, all giving off divine energy.

Father Theo invited me to go on one of his desert retreats. After my "orientation" to see if I could do it, he drove me across the peninsula to the other side–the Pacific Ocean side–to Kennedy's Bay. I was to live alone for a week in Dr. Arey's hermitage.

The log cabin had neither running water nor electricity. It was heated by an antique wood stove. (E) A cistern outside caught rain water. There was no toilet. I had to go out in the bush, dig a hole with a shovel, and sit on a shaky little toilet stool.

Up the hill a few yards away was the chapel–a three-sided shed. Inside was a beautifully carved little tabernacle (actually an ornate medicine cabinet). (F) It contained enough sacred hosts for me to go to communion every day. Father explained the schedule of readings, adoration and manual labor. He showed me how to dig a hole for a latrine and how to get the water. Some afternoons were to be spent in manual labor. My task was to dig up or chop down the blackberry bushes which were "intense." He explained that my adoration time was to be up in the shed overlooking the ocean and in the presence of the Blessed Sacrament.

The desert retreat was an incredible experience for me. Father Theo came out midway through the week to be sure I hadn't gone crazy. My retreat was wonderful, absolutely wonderful.

At the end of the first day, I wrote that I felt at peace about my tears. I had cried a lot about eventually having to leave the Coromandel, the Briers, Mabs, Father Theo and Joe. Their lives would go on separate from mine and I would not share their futures. But sad is not bad. I gave myself peace in feeling sad and about passing through the death of this separation. Then God spoke "I am your Eternal Center, always faithful, always in your center. I give you gifts of people for a while and you move through their lives. It's ok to be attached to each one. You are only embarrassed by your tears because people around you have not understood your tears and you always want to please. Try to please me and your tears are not displeasing to me. I'm your mother-father, the one who understands. I give you peace in the midst of your tears. I have given you each person in the Coromandel and in New Zealand to treasure and to be attached to, and I love your tears."

At the end of the second day, I wrote: "This was a strange day. Lots of distractions and anger, and I pray for humility, down-to-earthness, not to be lording it over, but to be real in my life, close to the earth." Here are some thoughts that struck me: "I am on my way to the wonderful tent, to the house of God, amid cries of joy and praise and the exultant throng. We could say much more and still fall short. To put it concisely: He is all, God is all." Emotional letting go was difficult for me. It had to be coupled with the gift of faith.

On the third day, I thought of Psalm 23. "The waters of repose revive my soul." I wrote to God, "I need these moments of repose as opposed to confusion, fear and turmoil. I need to be revived daily. Fear of not pleasing, fear of not being perfect, of not accomplishing, is what disquiets me. The opposite of this fear is resting in your arms, not reacting to others' opinions. You are the only one who counts. This is how I feel right now out here at Kennedy's Bay. One of my fears, God, is that I will lose so much when I go back to the United States."

God spoke, "You will never lose Me, no matter what. I am with you always. I have given you the New Zealand experience so that you will always know that I am with you. My goodness and kindness pursue you every moment of your life. I am your home as long as you live. And, YOU ARE MY HOME."

"YOU ARE MY HOME" was the great insight of that day, of my life. I was deep in adoration, prostrate with my feet actually outside of the shed, and it started raining and my feet got wet.

I turned around and saw a huge double rainbow over the Pacific Ocean. The reading that I had just done was, "We (the Trinity) will make our home with you..." and the deep understanding I had was, YES, GOD LIVES IN ME. He makes me His home, and wherever I am, with God in me, is home, even though it might not be in New Zealand. I felt very serene. In that prostrate adoration, with my feet cooled in the rain, that was true adoration in the hermitage shed, with the Eucharist in the little medicine cabinet tabernacle.

The next morning, the sunrise was at 6:30 over the Pacific. A cover of low pink clouds cast puffs of haze over the ocean and mountain islands. Then all the Tea trees came alive with droplets of rain from the night. Each leaf picked up the sun's glow. The splendor of the sunrise lasted a long time as the sun passed through several layers of clouds. (G)

My mind was exploding with thoughts. I walked down the road to assimilate the waves of the ocean caressing the little rock formations offshore. I thought of Matthew Fox's "God is an immense ocean in which we live." And from the Acts of the Apostles, "In God we live and move and have our being." God spoke to me through water. "God, you surround me as a mother's womb. I live in you. I am washed by you and strengthened by you."

I walked back to the hermitage, and discovered another friendly bull close to the cabin. Because I was afraid, I watched it from the porch, drinking coffee.

I tried to recall the wonderful phrase from Gerard Manley Hopkins about "Christ Eastering in us, with every sunrise." I had had this quotation on my wall for years, but just then I couldn't recall it. I wrote, "Easter is the pivot of the world and human history and my personal history. I am nothing. I owe all my existence to others, to God, to my parents. My cooperation, by letting go, is essential. **Life is a continuous letting go, sinking into the divine as into the ocean of unconditional love. Your death, Jesus, was a sinking into the divine, sinking and being immersed into dying for resurrection.**"

I meditated on the "remnant" which meant for me all peoples over the earth who love peace, simple living, sharing and supporting one another. I understood the covenant as God's unconditional love for us and our response as loving Him above all. Love, not guilt, had to become my motivation.

On the last day of the retreat, I cleaned the place up and aired and shook out all the blankets, and then at ten o'clock, Father Theo came to get me. We unloaded the bricks that he had brought for the wall he was building for an outdoor barbecue pit. The drive back was simply gorgeous.

We stopped to pick Ponga branches to use as palms for that night which was Palm Sunday. We walked into a lovely old overgrown lane and found some young green ones. Then we stopped at the summit and looked out over Coromandel Bay, the Firth of Thames, and on the other side, the Pacific Ocean and Kennedy's Bay. We could see the river valley going into the Pacific, the islands on both sides, Tea trees, and green pastures and the little Coromandel Township nestled in the lower hills. To me it was one of the most beautiful spots on earth.

We arrived back Saturday in time for the evening Vigil of Palm Sunday with the blessing of the Ponga branches in the garden outside the church. The children received the Ponga first and then we processed over to the church. John Brier and Father Theo and Keith read the Passion according to Saint Mark. It was well done. Afterwards I asked to go and see the sunset on the west side of the Coromandel, since I had seen the sunrise that morning on the east side.

Palm Sunday afternoon, I finally found the quotation I had been looking for from "The Wreck of the Deutschland." "Let him Easter in us, be a Dayspring to the dimness of us. Be a crimson cresseted east." Palm Sunday had been a sunrise, sunset day–a fitting end to my retreat.

I returned to the Briers and my batch in time for a very special Holy Week. Father Theo wanted me to help him, because his parishioners had had no Vatican II update.

On Holy Thursday, we arranged the pews in church facing each other. Being very sensitive to the people, he had the washing of the hands instead of the feet. I dried their hands. I was touched. After Mass he enshrined the Blessed Sacrament in the middle between the pews facing each other. Many stayed watching and waiting with Our Lord. I was thinking back on my day. That was the day when I went to the tiptop of the farm and painted my first spontaneous watercolor. It was of the Hauraki Gulf with all the little islands and the mist surrounding them.

On Good Friday, the electric power in all of Coromandel mysteriously went out. Father Theo had made a cross from two Ponga trees and in silence and lit by candlelight, we slowly came forward to kiss the cross. When we got home after the service, we built a fire in the fireplace and roasted potatoes in the coals, cooked eggs on the butane burner and ate by candlelight. It seemed very appropriate for the darkness of Good Friday.

The Easter Vigil was extraordinary. We lit the blazing new fire in the garden. John Brier carried the Pascal candle and we all processed in. I read the Exultet. What a privilege! During the simplified, but complete Vigil, the children sat in front on the floor listening very attentively.

On Easter Sunday morning, Brandon, Gerard and Kelly helped me paint dozens of Easter eggs. After Father Theo finished his Easter service in Whitianga, he came over and hid the eggs. The Coromandel children came for an Easter egg hunt.

In the afternoon, I walked over to the paddock in front of the wool shed and sketched the gnarled exposed roots of the old Pahutukawa tree. (H) What a meditation! I just rested there and thought about my time with the Briers.

Many images in my mind stood out. One was a lovely waterfall which plunged into a small pool where I swam and sketched. Another was walking late at night on the road under the stars whose brilliance was undiminished by city lights. One night I rushed back and painted a shooting star piercing the dark, diamond clustered sky.

I had an extremely hard time leaving the Briers. Since childhood, I have suffered from separation anxiety. When I left Belgium, after my novitiate, I experienced heart- wrenching sorrow. Leaving the Briers felt the same. I cried for the last few days. Kelly had never seen anyone weep like that.

Leaving New Zealand

My trip from Coromandel back to Christchurch was an adventure of kindnesses from friends who took me just a bit further on my way. John's mother, Mary, had become my "mum" away from home. She helped me with my grief. On this rather long land and water trip from the northernmost part of New Zealand down to Christchurch, I experienced the connectedness of all of New Zealand.

My return to Christchurch coincided with Glenda's two month trip to the United States. She was Christchurch's Beginning Experience representative to the 1982 International Convention in Denver. I had agreed to stay during her absence with her son, John (age18) and her daughter, Jane (age16). I moved in a few days early for her orientation and was, I thought, well prepared for this job.

My stay with them started off with a bang. John fell off his motor bike when he hit a dog on the way to work. He was quite injured, having severely skinned his hand and knee, and needed to stay home for two weeks. Jane's friend, Lisa, arrived with her friend and another Lisa. I enjoyed John and Jane because of their sensitivity and freshness, but the two Lisa's were a pain. To everyone's relief, they finally left after Jane gave them a deadline.

John and Jane were a delight: John loved his music and talking to me and Jane was a friend to everyone. She was a good cook and fixed "deliciously brilliant" omelets for me and for Allison, who had just moved in. *Brilliant* was the word she used to describe anything she liked. Allison, a 16 year-old punk-rocker, had recently come over from England. She soon became John's girl friend. She was a sensitive, helpful young woman and I was glad she was around.

Jane and Allison took the dog, Harriott, to the vet's because of a painful shoulder tumor, and the awful verdict was to have Harriott put down the next day. Jane cried and cried. That evening Allison's parents came for tea (dinner). With Jane's coaching, on how to prepare a roast dinner the New Zealand way, I made a delicious dinner. I was glad to meet Allison's parents–good solid people from England, and it was a lovely evening.

Allison stayed the night in order to go with me to take Harriott to the vet. Jane sobbed as she cuddled Harriott before we left for the 7:50 a.m. appointment. A friend drove us, with Allison sobbing by the time we got there. The vet picked Harriott up like a little lamb and talked to her until she died in his arms.

One reason I wanted to meet Allison's parents was because I was curious about punk-rockers. In addition John was a "boot boy." Boot boys had a reputation of being anarchists who got their kicks from smashing things and people. They were considered a violent, restless group of unemployed young men in New Zealand and in England. John and all his friends wore black boots, spiked belts, chains and had spiked hair or had Mohawks. John was the leader of the boot boys, which meant that the boot boys were at Glenda's house a lot. The group that came to Glenda's were not mean to me and were actually very considerate of me. They loved boot boy music, mostly anti-police, pro-IRA, and anarchist. John was such a gentle, kind and sensitive person; it was a mystery to me that he was the leader of the boot boys. Being with all of them, I had first hand knowledge of young people in New Zealand. Many of them lived for the moment: sex, cards, friends, smoking and beer. High unemployment and poor economic conditions fed into that.

I was determined to be understanding and yet to keep everyone safe. I had a meeting with them to make it clear that they were not to smoke pot or bring any drugs to the house. I explained that, if I suspected that they broke this rule, they would all be sent out and I'd call the police. They could, however, drink beer.

They had parties every weekend. The noise level was extreme. The beach was two blocks away, so I just escaped and went down to walk on the beach. They talked to me a lot and I learned of their frustrations and about their families. I knew that they were all wonderful young people.

Their goodness became clear to me. Glenda had planned to sell her house upon her return from the United States. It was a revelation to watch as these boys painted and wall-papered the interior of the house; as they poured a cement driveway and cleaned up the outside. When Glenda returned she put her house on the market and it sold.

Being with John and Jane and Allison and the boot boys opened a whole new world for me. I got to know them quite well and to see what they were up against in New Zealand. The punk rock movement came much earlier to New Zealand, England and Ireland than it came to the United States. I have had ever since then a soft place in my heart for young people who are doing strange things in the face of their insurmountable problems. (#s 20 and 22)

Before I left New Zealand, I arranged to splurge on a wonderful coach tour of the South Island. I was excited to go on the tour to see some of the famous scenic areas. I boarded the luxury bus along with forty other tourists from all over the world–Americans, Canadians, Japanese, Germans, and Italians. The trip from Christchurch to Dunedin was very icy. Just north of Dunedin, the reports were that the road was in "shocking" condition, but we got through. Since it was raining, we went directly to the hotel. I was the only single person on the tour, so I had my own room at each stop. The first one was teeny–a postage stamp room.

Two Canadian young women knocked on my door and we started our adventure for the evening. We found a place to eat lobster and later found the "dancing water fountains" in the city square. Next day, we set off for Te Anau. It rained all day. At Gore I bought two drawing pens to use in my sketch book. Then we were off again on an icy road. Every time we stopped, I sketched the scene out the window. I made a lovely collection of the sketches. For me, sketching was the best way to remember because the scene went into my eyes and mind and then flowed from my hand into the sketch.

We arrived at Te Anau and got settled in. That evening we saw magnificent films of the New Zealand fiordland area. I went to my room to absorb all that information about the Milford Sound and Queenstown. Next day we left for Milford. Again the weather conditions were icy. There was frost on the road going to the Homer Tunnel. The road through the native bush and beech forest was lovely–snow on every leaf and twig. We stopped at a lodge for morning tea and I sketched the bush. I had already sketched my first glimpse of the mitre type mountains in the distance. (Sketch I) They were the most spectacular mountains I had ever seen. As we got closer, the whole window was mountain. We were surrounded by snow but we triumphantly made it through the Homer Tunnel and cheered as we emerged.

In Milford Sound, we saw the haze-covered Mitre Peak and then it disappeared. Mitre Peak is the most famous mountain in this fiord. Because of the haze, the view was a bit disappointing, but the launch trip on the fiord was spectacular. There were hundreds of waterfalls. We rode in a glass-topped boat. We actually got right under the waterfalls. We could not only see them, but also be gushed by them. We got a much better view of Mitre Peak from the boat. The water of the fiord was so deep that it was jet black.

We arrived in Queenstown that evening. I had a wonderful sleep in my luxurious room. Next morning I threw open the drapes to behold the spectacular view of Lake Wakatipu and two ranges of snow-covered mountains–the Remarkables–descending into the water with their tops in the clouds. I was compelled, before dressing, or coffee, or even being fully awake, to sketch these "toe dipping" mountains. (J) I read from Psalm 108, "for your steadfast love is great above the nations, your faithfulness reaches to the clouds." That's it! God's steadfast love! God is the fiords and mountains stretching to the clouds. My theme for the rest of this trip and for my future was "God, your care for me is always near and I love you."

After spending the morning in Arrowtown, I got on the gondola and went up to the top of the mountain. I sat by the window in the lookout and sketched every part of what was below until it started snowing and I couldn't see. (K) Then a real miracle happened. The woman from Lubbock, a real American tourist, whom I had judged as a loud Texan, came over to me while I was sketching. She came over to talk and started weeping about the death of her husband. I reflected on how judgmental I had been. During our visit, I saw her in a different light and I hoped that I would not judge anyone again on externals.

I went back down on the gondola and walked around in the gentle falling snow. I found some seafood chowder and a Queenstown ski cap and walked back up the hill to our motel and sketched the view of the mountain in a different sunlight. That evening I watched television: *The Other Side of the Mountain*. I thought that was a fitting close to my Queenstown experience.

On the trip back to Christchurch, we went through the only industrialized part of New Zealand that I had seen. It was gray and desert-like, with lots of cement buildings. Seeing that industrial section showed me what manufacturing and industry can do to a beautiful land.

Toward the end of my time in New Zealand, I spent a weekend with Martin and Iwa Solomon. At the *Tangi* (funeral), Martin had explained to me the Maori burial customs. He told me that he was a crayfisherman (lobster fisherman) off the coast of Kaikoura. (*Kai* means "to eat" and *Koura* means "crayfish.") His Maori ancestors had fished off that coast for hundreds of years. He had invited me to come and experience the life of a crayfisherman, to go out with him to set the lobster traps at 1:00 a.m. and then to go with him at dawn to collect the lobsters.

A member of the Beginning Experience team who knew Martin took me there. We followed Martin's simple directions, "When you hit the sea, turn left" and we found their home. Once inside, we were warmly greeted by Martin and Iwa and their children and some friends. We walked down a long hall, with bedrooms on either side to the main room, where there was a blazing driftwood fire, some old lumpy chairs, comfortable cushions thrown all over and the television turned to the one and only channel, channel one. There were no arguments that way.

We sat down and I slowly began to connect which children belonged to whom and to enter into the conversation. It was a quiet atmosphere. Even the children were quiet.

The photographs on the wall were fascinating. Martin's mother, as a young girl, was beautiful. In the portrait of his mother and father they wore feather cloaks. On the opposite wall were people from France in business suits, one with his feather cloak over his suit. On that wall were portraits of his grandfather and his great grandfather, who was a Maori chief, with head feathers and a feathered cloak and with large bare feet.

We talked a long time. Martin went out alone in the rain to set the lobster baskets and next morning had returned with the lobsters before I got up. In their warm hospitality they had given us their beds, while they all slept on the floor.

When I went into the kitchen next morning, there was an enormous whole dead fish on the counter. Martin had caught it while bringing in the lobsters. The fish was breakfast. While they cooked it I saw the effortless Maori way of doing everything. There was lots of time to talk. They were busy but not hurried– intent on meeting our needs.

On Saturday, we met Sister Mary who had just returned from Rome. While in Rome, she had studied Eastern gifts to Christianity. She was teaching the people of Kaikoura centering prayer, eastern meditation and the importance of the Maori culture to Christianity. She explained that the common food cupboard that is found in a prominent place in all the Maori *Pa* (meeting places) is a sign of the Eucharist–the ever present gift of life.

Through the rich dialogue that day, I learned a great deal about the spirituality of Martin, Iwa and Sister Mary. Martin spoke: "We are all in the heart of God, created in the heart of God." I thought of the ocean of God's love. He continued, "We see only part of God. He is more infinite than our limited perception of him and he is bigger than our mistakes."

They demonstrated such an acceptance of the life-death cycle; the seasons, the earth, the mountains, the rivers and the sea. They had a calm acceptance, not a frantic fear of the future and what might happen.

On Sunday morning, we went to the cemetery. We climbed up the steep hill overlooking Kaikoura Bay where Martin's sister was buried under a simple wooden cross. Maori burial grounds were always on the highest hill overlooking the sea.

That cemetery was where Martin's parents and grandparents were buried. I prayed there on the mountain-top cemetery with all the ancestors, and I reflected on the fact that I knew where my grandparents were buried, but not my great grandparents or my great, great grandparents. The cemetery had generations of tombs in it. The ancient burial ground held the actual physical bones of all the ancestors of Martin and Iwa. I was in awe. What a marvelous way to end my time with them–reflecting with them in the midst of their long history.

I had intended to go crayfishing with Solomon. Though that never happened, something far better occurred. I was able to see into their lives and be with them in the midst of their ancestors. Martin went out alone in his little boat in the rain and put down all the traps as the Maori had done for centuries. Out on the horizon, we could see the Japanese tuna ships. The Japanese fish, then process and can all the tuna right off the coast of New Zealand. New Zealanders are angry about other countries coming and using the waters just outside the national line. The two exist side by side–the crayfishermen who have fished from their small boats for centuries and the Japanese in their large factory ships. That contrast spoke volumes to me.

After leaving Martin's home I returned to Christchurch and began letting go. I used every tool that I had learned from the Beginning Experience to close the door gently and firmly on this un-repeatable sabbatical year.

I had started by experiencing the effects of segregation and racism. I became committed to non-violence, to living in simplicity and to living one day at a time. I loved my sketching and was bringing back in my heart all the scenes I had sketched. I had lived with the extraordinary people of New Zealand, with the Maori and even with the punks and boot boys. I thanked God for all.

I said my goodbyes in the airport at Christchurch. As I flew north, I watched out my window as New Zealand went by. The whole east coast, Kaikoura, across to Nelson, the Marlborough Sound, Cook Strait, Mount Egmont, Auckland and the Coromandel off in the distance. It was like looking at a great relief map of New Zealand. Au Revoir.

CHAPTER 9

LIFE AFTER NEW ZEALAND

My sabbatical year in New Zealand was pivotal. In it I absorbed all that had gone into the creation of Beginning Experience. I had slowed down enough to deepen these realizations. I had listened to God. I had been transformed and renewed. **My conscious attention to living had confirmed in me the Beginning Experience process. Certain aspects stood out: letting go of fear, trusting God, being transformed by suffering, trusting the Holy Spirit in all encounters, writing to and from God, being a home for God, thanking God, reaching out, and being open to surprises.**

My return to the "real world" was gentle. I did not come directly back to the United States. Instead I flew across to Australia. I stayed with Beginning Experience team people on the east coast of Australia. I saw firsthand the expansion of our ministry. I praised God for the strength and love of those Australian pioneers and for Father Guy's direction.

My gentle return was deepened by the kindness of Father Guy who arranged his visit with the Hawaii team just at the time I was returning. A weekend took place on Oahu which I attended in order to let go of the past year and be ready for the future. Father Guy gave a talk, in which he said. "The one grace God will always give us, if we ask for it, is forgiveness–forgiveness for ourselves and the grace to forgive others." That was powerful for me.

After this memorable weekend, Father Guy gave us a grand tour of some of the other islands. (L) I was ready to return to the real world.

I flew from Hawaii to Albuquerque for a brief visit with my sister, Catharine. While there I went to her friend's book store to look for poetry by Gerard Manley Hopkins. When I tugged it from its place on the shelf, a book fell from the shelf above and hit me on the head. That book was *The Zen of Seeing, Seeing/Drawing as Meditation*, by Frederick Franck. I sat and read most of it right there. It immersed me in the way of "art as meditation." What a discovery, that my sketching was meditation!

From Albuquerque I went to Fort Worth, where I was welcomed at Holy Name Convent by wonderful Sisters of Saint Mary. I lived in a great parish with vibrant liturgies and outreach to all. After Christmas, I went to work across the street at Saint Theresa's Home, a residential home for emotionally and physically abused children in grief. I worked with the staff on group skills which they used with their children who lived in "family" groups. That experience was my first exposure to abused children and the devastating wounds of abuse.

Among the volunteers were young women, Volunteers in Education and Social Service (VESS), who lived in community. They gave their youthful dreaming and energy to the children. They were also learning how to live in and create community. I facilitated a weekly discussion group for them about living in harmony with each other. We used Jean Vanier's *Community and Growth*, which described L'Arche as a community providing home for people with developmental disabilities. I saw how L'Arche nurtured life among people with developmental disabilities and young volunteers. In Vanier's book, he emphasized that forgiveness is the foundation of all relationships since no one is perfect and we all hurt one another. I was connected back to Father Guy's words about forgiveness and connected to a future, yet unknown to me, my future work in L'Arche.

At this point, though, I did not know what I wanted to do "when I grew up." God guided me through a significant retreat which helped me be open to the future.

On May 19, 1983, Sister Ginny Vissing, Edith Honkomp, who had just been diagnosed with cancer, and I drove from Fort Worth to the Jesuit Spirituality Center in Grand Couteau, Louisiana.

Grand Couteau was a sacred place for me. My grandmother, Josephine Eugenie Mouton, after whom I was named, went there to Sacred Heart Academy. That academy was one mile from the Jesuit Spirituality Center down a lane of arching Live Oaks, called "Oak Alley." I could picture my little grandmother walking under that arch of Live Oaks.

The grounds of the Jesuit Spirituality Center were beautiful. That first evening after supper I went out and lay under a Live Oak and watched the gentle movement of the leaves and listened to the myriad kinds of birds. That retreat would be a turning point into a new phase of my life. I recorded much that God spoke to me:

+ *It's not important to have lots, but to be thirsty for life–for adventure with God.*

+ *I swim in the ocean of God's love with buoyancy and peace.*

+ *On the Our Father: Calling God Abba, I ask that His name be held holy, cherished, clasped close, held up, that His name be sacredly held.*

+ *On Psalm 139: I love the expression of creation, "put me together in my mother's womb" and I thought of all the "put-me-togethers-in-the-wombs of all the women" in my ancestry near here–near Grand Couteau.*

+ *I have faith because I can look back on all God has done, all His faithfulness to me.'*

+ *Reflection on the lilies of the field: "That is why I'm telling you not to worry, because God cares for you more than the birds of the air and the lilies of the field." It has pleased the Father to give me the Kingdom. God delights in me. The two main messages of Jesus are: to trust God and to forgive. I remembered the explanation of Anthony de Mello that I had heard the year before: all our sins could be drowned in a teacup. God forgives and forgets. He does not even remember our sins. "He wouldn't know what we were talking about." They are in the ocean of His love.*

+ *Pentecost was the third day of this retreat. I reflected on all creatures: "As a grain of dust that tips the scales, like a drop of morning dew." The paradox is that we are all nothing; that is, we came into being by Your Power from nothing, You hold all in existence by dwelling "in." Your imperishable Spirit is in all. I am capable of being hospitable to the Spirit of God. My joyful task is to be hostess to God–to be His dwelling place for His imperishable Spirit.*

On that Pentecost day I sat in the grass under a Live Oak and sketched the little church with its steeple "held" between the trunks of two arching oaks. At the end of the sketching, it began to rain. (M)

+ *One morning right after I woke up I had the incredible thought: "They crucified Him. How did that happen, that they considered Him to be so evil, that they crucified Him?" They were looking for someone else, and so they did not recognize him. But to crucify Him, that was so extreme. Yes, it was an attempt to eradicate the Life of the world. The paradox remained that, in His dying His life was ensured through all ages. His plunge into death revealed the total power of God.*

+ *I was present at the Last Supper and nestled into Jesus and heard Him say, "All I ask of you is forever to remember me as loving you." And I realized that was a two-way conversation" Jesus saying that to me and me saying to Jesus, "Remember me as loving you."*

+ *I realized that when I focus on my faults or my goodness, I miss seeing God. I understood that God is constant; my faithfulness is intermittent, and that's OK. I'm emerging into faith and love. God's constancy and faithfulness is what is important.*

+ *I no longer focused on my efforts at goodness and perfection, but on being captured by Christ Jesus.*

After this retreat we drove back the 10-hour drive from Grand Couteau to Fort Worth. We talked about what we had gained from this retreat. Edith especially shared and even said, "I'm ready to go now." She died within the year.

That retreat was a superb preparation for my future. But a surprise was waiting for me. In June several of us from Holy Name packed up to go on a beach vacation in Galveston. Our plans were cut short just as we got onto Galveston Island. We were smashed from the rear by a fully-loaded American Rice 18-wheel truck. The watermelon in the cooler was splattered all over the van, the seats were all broken, and we were taken briefly to the Emergency Room at Saint Mary's Hospital in Galveston. Our driver had severe whiplash and we were pretty shaken up. We returned to Houston and never finished our vacation.

While in Houston, we attended Mass at Casa de Esperanza (House of Hope). Our sisters had two homes for abused and neglected children whose parents had placed them in our care. All the children, staff and volunteers gathered on the floor around the altar. The priest drew everyone into the liturgy. There was dancing, singing, joy and love. I was immediately drawn to that place and wanted to be part of it. The American Rice truck had spun me around into a new direction. In September, I returned to Casa.

On my first day there I opened my spiral notebook ready to observe and take notes. I soon learned to loosen up and get into the spontaneity of each moment at Casa. I eventually became the Volunteer Coordinator, I think, because it took me a while to "get it." At this job I obtained volunteers and then trained them and walked with them in their care for the children.

Casa bought an old home on Hopkins Street and my friend Vicky and I lived upstairs as housemothers for two of the Casa families downstairs. One morning we heard some commotion downstairs and I went down to see what it was. A man was in bed with one of our mothers. I stood above them and ordered him out. He didn't move. I soon realized he didn't have a stitch on. So I left and so did he. This may sound crude, but I went back upstairs and said to Vicky, "It looks like 'pussy' rules the world."

I was so frustrated, saying to myself, "Look at all we've done for you: a place to live, business school, Montessori for your children, bicycles, typewriters, and on and on." I was beginning, just beginning, to realize that changing the cycle of violence and reversing the strong cultural influence for our mothers at Casa would take a long, sustained time. I also realized that it was not about us giving them something or doing something for them. They had to be convinced themselves and the actions had to come from them. For each mother, this meant changing not only life-long, but generations-long cultural patterns. That would require much time, concentrated effort and our loving, not patronizing, support. We were there to assist and guide.

At Casa, I appreciated anew the process of the Beginning Experience which had been designed to help grieving people let go of the past, move through grief and start new lives free from violence. The reality of abuse sank deep in my heart. I began to understand the struggles of single parents and the impact of generations of repeated violence that brought people to abuse their children.

I loved my life at Casa. And, most of all, I loved the children. However, at the end of two years I wanted a slower pace. I wanted to get back to counseling one-on-one. Casa found someone who wanted my job and Sister Mary Irma was to be living alone on the coast in Lake Jackson. Since being close to the beach and the Gulf of Mexico was high on my list of priorities, I asked her it I could come live with her. She was pleased to welcome me.

I moved from Casa de Esperanza to Lake Jackson in the summer of 1987. Sister Mary Irma and I started our community life together by making a beach retreat at a "stilt" house on Galveston Island. We had a little altar decorated with sea shells. I sketched and journaled and we prayed together and got to know each other.

After our retreat we settled into our life in a lovely home rented from Adele Savasso whose husband and two children had died. She eventually became a team member on the Houston Beginning Experience team. Her husband had said that he wanted to have sisters live in his house. That home was where I set up my private counseling practice.

God guided me into concerns for Central America at a time of violent persecutions of peasant farmers. Millions of people attempted escape to "el Norte."

In the winter of 1988 Sister Mary Irma and I went to the Rio Grande Valley to take part in the "Border Witness" program. That particular year was the height of the passage of millions of people fleeing from the killings in El Salvador, Honduras, Nicaragua and Guatemala. Our sisters from the Eastern Province had been in the Valley for several years working in *El Corallon*, the prison where illegal immigrants were held until trial and deportation back to their countries. The Border Witness Program provided hands on education of the awful plight of Central Americans escaping the life-threatening dangers in their homelands. We visited local communities of Salvadorans who were farming and living as they did in El Salvador. Their joy and hospitality spoke to me of the Body of Christ. They were living Christ's life, suffering, death and resurrection.

During our short time there, we were immersed in prayer, community, refugee camps, trial courts, legal offices, scrap-tent villages and transporting refugees. Our minds and hearts opened to what was going on so close to us at the Rio Grande River. That black page in history remained imbedded deep inside of me.

When I returned to Lake Jackson I started a Central American Concerns Study Group. We met at the Lutheran church. I knew from my involvement with Beginning Experience that group study and sharing was the best way to come to know anything. We started by reading *Bitter Fruit*, the historical account of the takeover of the Guatemalan government in 1954. The fall of that government was the result of the powerful influence of the United States, in trying to control the banana plantations. That book helped educate us. We then used newspaper and magazine articles to provide an understanding of what was taking place just south of us.

Our parish youth group went for a Border Witness experience. They came back with transformed hearts toward those escaping torture and death. Dole Bananas came weekly into our port from Honduras. The containers of bananas were then shipped throughout the central part of the United States. So Lake Jackson had a special connection to Central America.

The study group provided a means of research into the causes of this terrible clash between the very poor peasants who owned small farms, and those who wanted to have all the power and land.

We were also doers. One of our projects was the making of solar cookers to send to Honduras. DOW Chemical plant employees were in our group and they got the company to produce roofing materials made from discarded tires. DOW made plastic containers to store tomatoes grown in Central America and then they shipped the tomatoes to Italy for manufacture into sauce. The Lutheran Congregation in whose church we met became a twin parish to a church in Honduras. The sharing between those churches was two way: both giving and receiving.

Thus was born my deep and abiding heart connection to Central America. Oscar Romero, the slain bishop of El Salvador, and Rigoberta Menchu, the Guatemala woman who exposed the atrocities of the army, became heroes for me.

Another group I started was the Alzheimer and Mentally Ill Caregivers' Support Group. One of my clients was married to a woman who had been mentally ill, since the birth of their second child. For many years, she had lived in the house, never leaving and eating only white bread and bananas. He needed support in this difficult situation. Another client's husband was in the end stages of Alzheimer's. I asked if the three of us could meet together for support. They talked and listened to each other and we read part of *Thirty Six Hour Day*. Then others joined the group. It soon became older men and women whose spouses had Alzheimer's, and younger parents whose teenage sons or daughters were on drugs or had adolescent schizophrenia. We found resources, but most of all the weekly sessions provided support. The seasoned members listened and gave their valuable wisdom and love for the newer ones.

While I was in Lake Jackson, I was a Hospice volunteer. Because of my involvement with dying cancer patients but mostly because of Jo Lamia's death (see Chapter 10), I saw a need for a Cancer Support Group. So I invited several cancer patients to come. We used Bernie Siegel's *Exceptional Cancer Patient* materials. I knew that those meditations eased the pain and gave serenity to the men and women who came. That was the saddest group to be with, because so many died. Actually, the entire first group died. We re-started with the help of the hospital and finally moved to the cancer center.

With all those groups, I experienced again and again the unique value of sharing in groups where the whole becomes more than the sum of its parts. I understood that something mysterious happens when two or three gather together. A spark is ignited. The Holy Spirit emerges in the midst of the group. From my very first time to be in a small group on the Happening, to the Engaged Encounter when Jo Lamia and I shared our inmost thoughts and feelings, to the countless times of being in Beginning Experience groups, I learned over and over again the value of groups. I was always awed by the workings of the Holy Spirit. The WOW! never lessened. I believed that God was "in the in between" (Rosemary Haughton).

On the lighter side, I actually learned to paint with watercolors. I took a weekly class at the art museum, learning all the techniques of watercolor. More importantly, I developed a great love for seeing the spaces, colors, shades, grandeur and detail in nature. The world around me came alive. Watercolor was more transportable than oils, and I often took my paints, brushes, paper block and pen for an adventure of sketching and painting.

The ocean–really the Gulf of Mexico–was minutes away, so I went often to walk the beach, collecting shells. Lightning Welks and Scallops were my favorites. I learned to ride the waves and to body surf. I spent hours in the ocean of God's love. **Riding the waves became a deep physical experience of letting go, sinking into and riding on God's love.**

Sister Mary Irma was called to another ministry. Before she left we had decided that our house and a beach house would be used for retreats. She had given me some great ideas for retreats. "A Day at the Beach" retreat was about being in touch with all aspects of the beach. It used three one-hour intervals of meditation and mindfulness focusing on the waves, sand, and shells. When I used this retreat for myself I discovered all the sounds of the waves. The crashing powerful sounds were evident, but the gentle hissing and rolling sounds were not so evident. I used that retreat with many who came to Lake Jackson for a time way from their busy lives.

I also offered the "Faith and Community" weekend to groups. That retreat became a time of going back to one's faith roots, of faith experiences in childhood and throughout life, and ending with the affirmation of Christ living within. I loved giving these retreats mostly to Beginning Experience people and church groups

In addition to the retreats and study groups, I continued counseling. I was however stalked by someone who was a drug addict. He was angry with me for refusing to work with him as long as he was using drugs. I felt terrorized. A friend of mine was moving from her home to an apartment where she was not allowed to have her Bassett Hound, a big puppy named Dumplin'. So she offered Dumplin' to me as a guard dog. I called this arrangement my "rent a dog." (#23)

Dumplin' sounded ferocious with her deep, loud bark. We had an altercation with the neighbor behind us about this bark. All ended well, even though I had feared having to give her up. Eventually the stalker moved away.

I brought Dumplin' into the kitchen at night to have her sleep behind a movable barricade. I felt very safe and the neighbor was spared her night barking. I honestly thought she would protect me. We were very much alike. She snored as loud as I did. One night I awoke. Dumplin' was still snoring, fast asleep. Red and blue lights were flashing all around and I peered through the front blinds to see a fire truck and six police cars in front. Dumplin' snored on and never awoke. I ventured out to see what was happening. Some vandals had set fire to all the cars parked on the street.

I never woke Dumplin' up or scolded her. I still believe that if someone had broken in she would have put up a fuss. Just having her–sweet Dumplin'–near by was comfort to me.

While in Lake Jackson, in the midst of all my concerns I went to Guatemala. Father Guy had finished his term as Executive Director of Beginning Experience and after a sabbatical in Rome; he went to the Benedictine mission in Guatemala. He invited me to come visit.

CHAPTER 10

JO'S DEATH

In between Casa de Esperanza and Lake Jackson, an event of great impact occurred. Jo Lamia died.

On May 10, 1986, Jo called me at Casa. I was standing in the yellow kitchen at the Hyde Park children's home. "Josephine, I've got the Big C." Her voice cracked. "And the doctor says I have a year." I heard those words and I heard the fear she didn't say. I was shocked. I was angry at that doctor for telling her so soon that she had only a year. I hated being so far away.

My friendship with Jo had begun on the Happening Team. Her exuberant joy, deep faith in God, and love of people had brought life to that ministry. I loved her like a sister. She was more than a friend. She was co-creator, with God through me of this marvel–the Beginning Experience. I had spent every Tuesday night at Jo's where we had talked and had fun together.

During the growth years of the Beginning Experience, we had traveled all over the United States and had gone together to Hawaii, Australia and New Zealand. We had always been booked in the same room at the international conventions.

She attended her last Beginning Experience International Convention in New Orleans in July 1986. She was ill most of the time. A wonderful nurse on the Mobile, Alabama, team lovingly took care of her.

Jo never lost her sense of humor. I had given her a packaged assortment of sea shells from "my beach" which she had slipped into her suitcase. Later she opened her suitcase and said, "Something smells like tuna in here." She aired out her clothes, laughing all the time, and I sanitized the shells.

She was able to go to the French Quarter for a night out, listening to jazz, dancing and being photographed with people from around the world. By that time I had moved from shock to denial. I could not imagine life without her.

In August, she returned to teaching. She taught until Thanksgiving vacation, intending to resume with her beloved students after the holiday. She became quite ill and was in a lot of pain. Cancer was widespread in her bones.

I went up to spend time with her before Christmas. I was shocked to see how thin she had gotten since July. Her camel's hair winter coat hung from bony shoulders. Her hands were emaciated. Her face was gaunt.

She was surrounded by dear friends. She was determined to go to California for Christmas to be with her sons, Kevin and Mark. We did everything to conserve her energy, to build her up and get her ready for this trip. She did go; so did her ex-husband and his wife, Gay. Jo became very ill while she was there.

In February, I went to visit her again. She was failing fast. After that I came back to Fort Worth for a Sister of Saint Mary Assembly scheduled from March 6 to 8. On Saturday, I phoned and learned that Jo was going down fast. I begged Carmen Faracklas to let me come and stay. Carmen was her long-time friend who had come from New Mexico to live with her and care for her. She gave strict orders about how long people could stay, or if they could come at all. She let me come.

I went to Jo's on Monday, March 9. She didn't go to her scheduled doctor's appointment that day and went instead on Tuesday. He told her she was moving into the "invalid" stage. Her hypnotherapist was doing hypnosis on the phone. The hospice nurse said she could die at any time. Jo said she wasn't ready because she "wanted to be at her sons' (upcoming) weddings." She became very agitated and panicky. I talked to her hypnotherapist to learn what anchor and what words to use with her. I used my skills in hypnotherapy to bring her into an altered state and repeated over and over, "You are secure, unafraid and free of pain." Thank God that worked beautifully.

At that point I shut down emotionally. I knew that I had a job to do, that I had to be strong and I did not want to face that Jo was the one dying. I went into a sort of auto-pilot, not thinking or feeling, only recording in my journal and guiding the hypnosis.

Her son, Kevin, came on Friday, March 13. She dreamed that she had gone back to school to see all the children and that morning she stopped breathing and almost died. Her students at Saint Cecilia's had sent a long poster which was on her wall around the room. It read, "Happy Spring, Mrs. Lamia. We miss you, Mrs. Lamia." One child had drawn a painting of the sun in tears. Jo's other son, Mark, came on Saturday, March 14. The hospice nurse decided to take Jo off the medication that was causing her to be agitated and she became much calmer.

Mark and Kevin were so loving. They kept her comfortable with cold cloths and chipped ice. I can still see them stooping over her bed changing her cold wash cloths, putting them in different shapes and saying, "This one is the 'Queen Elizabeth fold' or the 'King George fold'" and her laughing.

Mark and Kevin heroically released her Saturday afternoon when they told her she didn't have to go to their weddings, that she could see them from heaven. Then she let go. Her concern had been that their brides would cry at their weddings. She said, "I'll find a handsome man in heaven to dance with and my legs won't hurt and I'll have hair."

On Sunday morning, she said her goodbyes. Carmen had the presence of mind to tape them for her family. After she finished, she threw herself back to die and went to sleep. When she woke up she said, "Oh, God I'm still alive." Her ex-husband, Peter, and his wife, Gay, were there most of Sunday. Jo loved Gay and Gay loved Jo. Jo gave her some advice on how to handle Peter. It was such a great scene around her bed, seeing Jo's love for those close to her, including her former husband and his wife. On her death bed, she was sending out healing energy and reconciliation to those around her.

The hospice nurse who had been there for eight hours came back Monday afternoon for another eight hours. She was so taken by Jo, and stayed until Jo died. On Monday Jo relaxed more and more. That evening she took some Jell-O with morphine and spoke her last words: "That's good."

Her breathing changed and I ran down the hall to get Mark. She died taking two short breaths. During her dying her body had been translucent, her skin paper thin. When she died her body became frozen, absolutely still. It was evident that her soul had left her lifeless body.

She died at 11:10 p.m. Monday, March 16. At that moment there was a terrific thunderstorm and a huge clap of thunder. The shuttered window blew open from the wind suction.

Father Rick from the church came and we all prayed around her body before the funeral attendants came to take her. Then we stayed up 'til after 4:00 a.m. telling Jo stories and "decompressing."

One of Kevin's friends came in the next morning and related the following: He was driving to Dallas to see Mrs. Lamia. He had a trailer hitched to his truck and the storm was so blinding he couldn't see. He saw Jo's face ahead of him and decided to pull over. The trailer came unhitched. It would have caused a wreck on the highway if he had not pulled over. He could hardly wait to tell us about this "miracle." Jo became instantly our patron saint.

I had no clothes to wear for her funeral so I went to the thrift store where they were having a Saint Patrick's Day sale and got all that I needed. Jo must have been chuckling. She always dressed so finely and here I was in second-hand-on-sale-clothes going to her funeral. There were two funerals, one for the school and one for the rest of us. Sister Tarianne de Yonker the new Executive Director of Beginning Experience came.

During her dying, Jo demonstrated her legacy. It was love: love for her sons –they meant everything to her–her friends, and the students she taught. She spoke of that loving as she was dying. She was grateful to each one of us and thanked us. At one point she said to the hospice nurse, "I want you to know how much I appreciate your teaching me how to breathe." She thanked Carmen for keeping her comfortable and happy and "up." She thanked me for staying at night. She was unselfconscious, meaning she was just herself. She could be mad at God for not coming sooner. She could tell Gay in front of Peter how to tell him off. She was concerned about how much we were giving up to stay with her and she was concerned about causing us suffering. She was aware of everyone around her and all that was happening.

I just couldn't cry, but after I went back to Lake Jackson I entered into my grief. I wrote to and from her. She said, "I told you I would speak and that you would be able to hear if you would listen...I will help you...use my face as your anchor."

It is still my anchor.

CHAPTER 11

GUATEMALA

Martha Freckleton from Beginning Experience in England and I went to Guatemala in 1989. I was plunged for a brief moment into the eternal mystery of Christ's suffering, death and resurrection. I wanted to keep in mind this great mystery of faith so I wrote these thoughts:

Guatemalans showed me the rising that can occur inside suffering and death, in the same mysterious way that Jesus contained the resurrection in the midst of his suffering and death.

I saw no despair, only the eternal hope that death did not have the last word. I saw in Guatemala that evil never conquers; it only seemed to conquer. The real–the living Christ-power–lay in the silent patience of the poor.

What struck me was the contrast between the armed-ready-to-strike-military of Guatemala and the serene patient-walking-power of the peasants.

I saw, heard, felt Christ in the people and in an alive Church. There was deep serenity, joy and hope, but no despair. There was, as well, incredible pain.

As we flew into Guatemala City we saw it spread out like a huge patchwork quilt of white and pastels with one bridge over the gorge of a river.

When we arrived a smiling Father Guy met us. (#24) He drove us through the city along the ancient aqueduct. Battle-fatigue-clad soldiers walked on top. Military were everywhere, all young boys who had joined the army because there was nothing else to do. They went into the army, often turning on their own people. Traffic was wild and pollution rampant, because there was no regulation.

We stayed at a beautiful little hotel. After dinner, we encountered a tiny girl about four years old who sold roses at the entrance of the restaurant. She and her brother (a bit older) were always there, sleeping on a mat on the curb. (#25) There was no sign of a mother. I will never forget her. Father Guy bought us roses and I still have the petals in my Guatemala journal.

I awoke the next morning to the singing of birds. Our next room neighbors were two women from *Heal the Children*.

Because we hadn't changed our clocks we arrived an hour early to meet Father Guy. We had the most delicious cups of Guatemalan coffee. We "did" Guatemala City as tourists. We started by going to a park where we studied an enormous relief map of Guatemala. We could see the high mountains, the volcanoes, some active and some extinct, the craters forming lakes, the lowlands, the oil fields, the jungle, the Mayan pyramid ruins, the borders of El Salvador and Honduras and Mexico, the Caribbean and Pacific Oceans. The rivers were running with water. This was an excellent preview of where we would go.

We could see Coban, the location of the Benedictine Priory. Father Guy outlined the Benedictine parish which extended north to the jungle. There was a refugee camp for the people of Quiche' inside this parish, and some of the oil fields were in the parish.

As we looked down from the observation tower, a group of children dressed in brilliantly colored skirts and tops came. They were very quiet and giggled when I took their picture. As with the refugees in the Rio Grande Valley, I was struck by their silence, humility and reserve–a tidal wave of silent humanity.

We found the restroom and got all wet. We had to "bucket" the flush. Then off to the artist market and after a few wrong turns, we found Museo Ixchel–the museum of the weaving of Guatemala. It was beyond superb. Mayan Indians had handed down their weaving from generation to generation. Weaving was done on primitive strap looms. I was enthralled by the museum which displayed the 5,000 distinct weaving patterns that exist in Guatemala.

We went to the big market. I felt guilty bargaining with the shopkeepers. All their articles were handmade and beautiful. Father Guy said, "You are no fun to shop with–they expect you to bargain." And so we did.

We returned to the hotel exhausted. Father Guy said Mass on the telephone table. It was the feast of Saint Mark. We prayed for Central America, especially the "disappeared" and all the peasants who were still suffering.

Next day we got up early and after breakfast–again the exquisite coffee–we started out for Solola and Lake Atitlan way up in the mountains west of Guatemala City. Here are my impressions as we drove: Lots of truck farms, brightly dressed peasants working the fields, brown denuded mountains, hard mountain driving with many curves, good "American built highway," many military and guerrillas, tiny men carrying huge loads of wood, and extreme poverty.

At one point, we stopped by the roadside to talk to a young mother with her three children. She simultaneously nursed the baby, wove on a handmade strap loom and sold melons. (#26) I will never forget her and her smile and humble quietness.

We only passed through Solola, an old (1547) city with great poverty and continued on to Lake Atitlan. The deep blue lake was the crater of an extinct volcano. Many tourists and hippies were at the market which was along the streets and on the rocky beach. The sellers were very aggressive.

On the way back, we headed to Antigua. We drove past terraced farms with colorful peasants working in the fields and the ever-present guerrillas who were armed and ready for battle. We talked about the peasants who were caught in between the military government and the guerrillas. One hundred thousand peasants had been killed by both.

We arrived in Antigua, an ancient city with many ruins due to a great earthquake in 1773 and another one in the 1970's.

It was in that city that every day, black veiled mothers walked around the plaza carrying pictures of their sons who had disappeared into the military trucks which had come and carried them off to the army. What deep and inconsolable grief for their mothers! While in Guatemala, we saw many icons of Our Lady carrying a picture of her son Jesus.

We returned to Guatemala City and prepared to leave the next morning for the Benedictine Priory in Coban where Father Guy was the interim prior. The journey north took us through the city. We passed miles of squalor, tin and cardboard houses and mountains of trash. Out of the city we drove through parched land and came to the bridge crossing the gorge, which we had seen from the airplane. That bridge was the place the guerrillas dumped bodies and Father Guy said he'd seen two bodies there recently.

We entered a land of tropical beauty. We stopped at the Quitsal Bird sanctuary up in the mountains, with bougainvilleas, orchids, lush vegetation and crops of fern. The people were Ladino (mixed Indian and Spanish). On our way we stopped at a gleaming white shrine on a hill which was famous for its healing baths and pilgrims and, alas, as on many roads, staggering drunk peasants.

We arrived mid-afternoon into the town of Coban with its narrow rock streets and the Benedictine Priory. The community consisted of the professed monks, two novices, several candidates and then a wonderful assortment of people including young boys who came to learn Spanish and work on the plantation. They lived in a house next to the guest house. Every night, forty homeless people came to a pension house to spend the night, paying ten cents. Another woman came, simply saying, "I'm staying with you." A blind man also came and said, "I'm staying." The laundress, the cook and her mother lived at the Priory.

We went to Mass at the church which is the parish church. Father Guy said Mass in Spanish. The novices, candidates and the young boys sang beautifully. It reminded me of the harmony singing at the Oscar Romero refugee camp on the Rio Grande border.

My room in the guest house had walls of solid mahogany, which is native to Guatemala. There was no electricity, but there were thousands of fireflies. Through the open windows I could hear dogs, people, turkeys and roosters all night. I did not sleep. In the morning, there were firecrackers.

From the balcony outside my room I looked down on a beautiful expanse of enormous tropical plants. I'm not sure about the size of the property. It seemed to be a village.

In one corner was the parish church, San Marcos. On the opposite corner stood the old church, made into a renewal and retreat center. Behind this sat the parish offices, rooms for the cook, laundress, blind man, and the woman who "came to stay." Beyond that was the pension house. In the center stood the Priory building. Next to it was the Catechetical Center where catechists from all over the region came to be trained as teachers. In the middle spread the old plantation house which served as the guest house. Next to it and up to the parish church, stretched the plantation where sugar cane, coffee, bananas, beans, chili, lettuce and spices were grown. That was a true monastic village. I was so taken with it that I did a quick sketch.

The monks served those who came with counseling, spiritual direction, or with a place to spend the night. They oversaw the retreat activity and the catechetical work, and the farm, ran the parish, provided adult and children's religious education and offered hospitality for many. It was a place of refuge for those who just spontaneously came in. In addition there were the novices and the monks who prayed the Divine Office from Lauds in the morning to Compline at night. All were involved in vital work for the Church.

Technology at the Priory was first class. Father Bernadine had set up two huge cable television dishes. He got perfect reception from the United States. He was a ham operator as well. All that enhanced the catechetical and parish work of the monks. I thought back to Father Guy's showing us on the relief map the large extent of the parish boundaries which reached north to the jungle.

The Bishop of Coban, in his compassion, had established an internal refugee camp for the safety of the widows whose husbands had been killed and who had no family or safe place to go. Martha and I wanted to visit this refugee camp. It was located near the Priory, or so we were told. Brother Ramon, who spoke Quiche', was our guide.

We had many adventures trying to find the camp. Our pilgrimage was slow from the start because of a marathon being run on the main road out of town. Boys who were cooling the runners with containers of water were throwing the water on each other. I was impressed to find so many signs of play and fun in the midst of tragic suffering.

We had been directed to pass the airport. The road we took led us to a lovely church being built with an enclosed convent of Dominican Sisters. We stopped to chat. But it was not the right road. We tried another which led past a field where two tired women arranged banana leaves as little tents to protect the baby coffee plants. Growing coffee is slow and laborious.

The women directed us up another steep hill. We encountered, at the top, a machine-gun-toting guard who told us we were trespassing on his finca (plantation). The women we had seen were peasants working his land. We turned back and, at a fork in the road, a man carrying a machete said, "up there"–pointing to the highest hill yet. Father Guy got out and switched to four-wheel-drive. When we got to the top, we could hear the children's voices. We had arrived.

The camp consisted of a church, two large containers of clean water, an outdoor cooking area and several houses. The houses were dirt-floored, and corn was drying from the ceilings. Mats and simple beds were on the floors. All was very clean and tidy.

This community was situated above a valley of coffee and bananas. Most of the women worked down in Coban. Every morning, barefoot, they scurried to work along a foot path down to the town. They left one woman at home to care for the children.

We met Maria, age thirty, with five children. (#27) She had a broad smile and radiated peace. Her eyes were alive, and she looked intently and lovingly at each of us. One of her children was sickly, and Martha explained about his need to drink a lot of water. CARA, a Catholic research program, supplied clean water and cooking oil.

Maria was most amazing. She and the children were happy. They had lost everything and had come here to the refugee camp. They were living day to day in God's hands. I experienced such gentle, loving energy here. It was a place of love, safety, family, hope and resurrection. Maria thought that Father Guy was the bishop. We didn't let him forget that.

Our visit was all too short. I cried as we left–watching Maria and the children smile at us. I kept thanking God for the people of Guatemala, who lived the resurrection in the midst of suffering and dying.

When we got to the bottom of the hill and back to the main road, Father Guy tried to shift to regular drive. He was afraid of ruining the Priory's only good car. He tried every possible combination to get it into regular drive. We all tried. A passerby tried. So Brother Ramon went by bus into Coban to get help.

While we were waiting, we watched many women walk by who acted as if they were afraid of us. Perhaps they were surprised to see strangers. We could hear military maneuvers in the distance. After two hours, Brother Ramon returned with Brother Paul, who easily shifted the car into the proper gear. When we got back to the Priory we had a "light refreshment" of black beans, Central American thick corn tortillas and pineapple.

The day was far from over. After eating we went to the Coban hospital. The patients brought everything: beds, mats, linens, food and caregivers. The Sisters of Charity provided nursing staff. It was very primitive, but again a joyful place. Two women were in labor, attended by a young male intern who showed us the sterile kits of gowns and instruments. One woman was 18, delivering her first baby. I prayed with her and massaged her back. The other woman was a grandmother, delivering her ninth baby. Being with these two women in labor in those primitive conditions was shocking for Martha who was a midwife.

We went to the Benedictine Sisters' convent for Mass. It was a contemplative group which operated a printing press. Their work was important for the church in Guatemala, connecting the local church to the rest of Latin America. There were native novices and professed sisters. The dialogue homily was about peace and justice. One novice wore a T-shirt showing a body hanging over a barbed wire. In Portuguese it said, "You've taken our land, now you've taken us," referring to Brazil and its people.

Between all this, we visited a silver jewelry-making shop. Native jewelers were making delicate silver baubles and chains, unique to the area. It seemed to me that in Guatemala, art and beauty stood in stark contrast to machetes and machine guns. Brilliantly-colored handmade items for the home bring beauty, energy, joy, and peace. The pace of life is slow and meditative, which nurtures creativity. As we drove home, we reflected on our long day and all the people we had encountered.

That evening we got some firsthand insight into the violence in El Salvador. One of the novices was from El Salvador. I spoke to him and Brother Paul translated. I believe those images of death and violence are important in order to see a bit of what happened in the 80's in Central America.

The novice had moved from his village to the Jesuit University at the time of Archbishop Oscar Romero's assassination. He had attended the funeral and had been in the Plaza when many people, including his grandfather, had been killed.

He was aware that the military was supported by the United States. However, he was not aware of the presence of Communism. He said his people were ignorant of the East/West conflict–Communism vs. United States–going on in Latin America. The Salvadorans were caught up in fear, isolation and terror. They were confused because there were so many factions violently opposing each other.

The violence went back a long way. There was a massacre in 1932. The novice's mother remembered it; the heads of the slain were hung in trees. Just recently, when he was coming home one night using a flashlight, he saw bodies stacked up as a road block. He said that, in the past he would have been very upset, but people had become hardened to that kind of violence. A state of terror existed in which almost no one trusted anyone else. People were isolated and secretive about their thoughts and actions.

The El Salvadoran novice told all with little emotion. He explained that in the newspapers one often read, "There are three options: first, leave; second, join the Guerrillas; or third, get killed."

The novice's account showed the stark contrast between life in El Salvador and in the United States. Many in Central America are asking those "in the North" to wake up and see how ignorance and greed are contributing to such destruction and to find solutions by letting go of greed and entering into solidarity with those in Central America. They were asking us who came to visit to build a bridge of understanding.

We spent a day traveling in another direction to Carcha, toward the Mayan ruins in the jungle. On the way, we visited a nutrition center, staffed by native nuns. There, the babies and children are brought back from starvation to health in an atmosphere of joy and serenity.

Once in Carcha, we visited an interesting museum attached to the church. The pastor of the church created this museum. It presented Mayan pottery, dances, costumes, dress, flora and fauna of the area– the Alta Vera Paz.

We went to the market, not a tourist market, but the gathering place for peasants who came to sell and buy everything which included live turkeys, goats, and all the necessities of life. All items, except the goats, had been carried wrapped in colorful woven cloths on their heads and then displayed on the ground.

When we returned home, Martha, a midwife, gave a marvelous talk on the unique grief that accompanies the loss of a child. The room in the parish center was packed. There were many personal questions and a lively discussion. Martha was pleased to contribute something to the people there.

On our last day in Guatemala, I woke up to singing coming from the Renewal Center. People had spent the night in prayer and were greeting the dawn with beautiful harmonic singing. The praying church was alive here.

We drove out of town and Father Guy said Mass in the unfinished church at the cemetery. It was packed with families and decorated with gladiolas and cala lilies from the fields. The prayer of the faithful, the blessing of the children, and the sign of peace were all energetic. Brother Philip gave the homily in Quiche' speaking to the Indians that the word of God is not like taking a shower. Instead, it is like being immersed in a bath.

After Mass, we walked through the cemetery–the only one in the Coban area. It was a slice of life and death. As the Irish say, "a thin time" between heaven and earth.

Next day, we returned to Guatemala City and then back to Houston. On the plane home, I wrote some of my impressions: the ready, gentle smiles; the men carrying heavy loads of wood secured to their foreheads with straps; thatched huts, foot paths, walking little ones–the feet people, smiling, with shining eyes; many children, worried mothers; Father Guy blessing the children; the humble posture of prayer at Mass; the silence of the people and the children; brilliant colors of the women; a silent tidal wave of people starting over; a patience and endurance beyond our imagining; the ever present armed soldiers; life and death–part of each day; the Mayan simplicity and joy expressed in the weaving of color one thread at a time; the pottery, the basket making, the art and music. And I wrote my first poem:

THE GUATEMALA INDIAN WOMAN

A great dignity envelopes her.
Her feet are placed carefully
Her bare or sandaled brown feet
Placed carefully on the earth.
She is GRACE.
Not graceful; she is grace.
Her head is strong.

LETTING GO: THE WAY INTO ABUNDANCE

She carries her load
With dignity and grace.
Her load of woman's things,
Fruits, vegetables, a turkey,
Cloth, baskets, pots,
Wrapped in brightly woven fabric.
She is a work of art
In motion
And stillness.
Motion of rapidly moving
Carefully placed feet,
Motion of arms
Swinging in graceful half circles
Balancing her back, neck, head, held straight.
Her skirt is part of her.

CHAPTER 12

MAMA
Helen Buchanan Stewart

On July 15, 1990, as I was writing to and from God in my little chapel in Lake Jackson, I felt pressure on my left arm and shoulder, as if someone was leaning against me. I asked God in my writing, "Who is this?" The answer came, "It is your Uncle John." I began to write to Uncle John asking him why he was there with me. He said, "I've always loved you and looked after you, ever since you were a baby in El Paso. Your mother was very special to me."

On the spot, I made the decision to go to Lafayette, Louisiana and talk to Aunt Virginia about Uncle John's relationship with Mama when she was a little girl back on *Auchmar* farm. Aunt Virginia, known as "Mikie," and Mama were now the only two left of the 11 children, and Mikie was in a nursing home. I felt an urgency to act quickly to get an idea of what life was like at *Auchmar* and to get a mental picture of Uncle John who had just come to me.

I drove to Lafayette and went to see Mikie. I asked her if, the next day, I could make a tape recording of her telling me about life at *Auchmar*. After some hesitation and not really wanting to do this, she agreed. Next day I returned and taped two long sessions with her.

Mikie explained that Mama and Sophie, the two youngest Buchanans, needed a father. Mikie told me that Uncle John had become Mama and Sophie's "buddie" and he had spent long hours playing with them. In the cotton fields, Mama held his little finger as he lifted her jumping over the rows of cotton. I vividly pictured this tall man with his limp from polio and little Mama laughing and jumping with her "buddie."

Uncle John worked at McFadden's and delivered groceries in a horse-drawn truck. He came home for lunch every day and wrestled with Mama and Sophie on the front porch. Mama and Sophie sometimes squeezed the blackheads on his nose.

Mikie told other stories of their life: the big pecan trees, the huge wisteria that covered the length of the front porch, the outhouses, the "darkies" they played with who were children of the tenant farmers, Grandma shooting the coons who stole eggs from the chicken house, riding to school on the pony and going to church in the wagon through the mud.

Her voice and face became lively as she re-lived those stories. I was pleased that I had come and made the tapes. The next day, I said goodbye and then drove back to Lake Jackson.

I received a phone call when I got back telling me that Mikie had had a massive stroke. She died two weeks later, never having spoken another word. I had on tape her last words. What a miracle God had worked, that Uncle John had come to me, and that I had gone to be with Mikie and to tape her precious story.

Mama grieved deeply over the death of her sister Virginia. Every time I phoned her she cried and said, "I'm the only one left now."

On an intuitive hunch, I decided to fly on Christmas day to Albuquerque to see Mama. (#28) That Christmas, 1990, she gave each of us, her children, something from her childhood. I believe that she had a premonition of her sudden death which would come within a month. I guess, in my unconscious, I had the same premonition.

Mama gave me her geography school book. Inside were listed the names of her siblings crossed out. The book had been handed down from one to the next and her name, Helen Buchanan, was the last one. She also gave me a little black notebook with jottings of her life as a young mother. She had written the "cute sayings" of my brother Mack and me. She wrote in January, 1937, "Josephine was trying to argue with me after I had scolded her and she said 'Don't you know I haven't undisobeyed you?'" and about Mack: "Mack was selling me some apples and he said 'They are very nice and they are very 'expensible.'" In poetic prose, she recalled our trip to Lafayette with the sights and smells of spring. She described our trip back when our *Teraplane* car exploded and burned to the ground. I must have learned from her to keep a journal. I'm grateful to have this precious gift of her thoughts.

Even after my visit at Christmas, I wasn't prepared for the phone call from my brother, Charlie, telling me that Mama had serious heart problems and was in the hospital. He said I should come. Instead of making arrangements immediately, I went to lead the cancer support group's weekly meeting and sobbed all the way through it. When I got home, I asked a friend to come stay with me and I asked Adele, who owned the house and who worked at a travel agency, to get my ticket. She got it for the next morning and drove me to the airport in Houston.

I cried so hard that my face was disfigured. My brother-in-law met me at the airport and prepared me to see Mama. He told me what had happened.

Mama and Daddy had gone to their granddaughter Amy's wedding in Washington, D.C. On their way back they had a few hours in Chicago in between train connections. The first Gulf War started the day they were in Chicago. There were massive demonstrations on Wabash Avenue, with people lying on the road to block traffic. Mama, who had always been a pacifist, was very disturbed by the war and especially by being thrown into the middle of the demonstrations in Chicago.

When they got back to Albuquerque, she started looking after her neighbor and had just taken a casserole next door. The man across the street reported, "Helen looked shaky." Mama went home and the doorbell rang. The newspaper boy had come to say goodbye because he was going to the Gulf War. Mama went to the back room and Daddy heard her give a loud sigh. He called 911 and she was taken to Saint Joseph's Hospital. There she was put on life support even though she had signed several "Do Not Resuscitate" Living Wills at another hospital. I believe that her favorite saint, Joseph, wanted her in his care.

When I got to the hospital and saw her, I was horrified. The apparatus in her nose and mouth forced her to breathe. I took her hand and spoke to her. A little tear trickled from her left eye. I know that she knew I was there. I just had to get there before she died and God mercifully arranged that, because the ambulance had taken her to the "wrong" hospital where there was no "Do Not Resuscitate" order.

The family met with the Ethics Committee of the hospital asking to allow her to be taken off the ventilator. When they said "yes," the doctor came in and abruptly shut it off. I screamed at him, "Take it out of her nose and mouth so she can be comfortable." The nurse gently did that. Mama lived about three hours. During that time, we told stories about her when we were young. Daddy left saying, "This is exactly how I saw my mother die." He stayed as long as he could. I knew he was re-living those sad times when he was a boy.

One of the great stories about Mama that we told that day was when we had a "butler" named J.C. Mind you, we were very poor, but Mama needed help cleaning, so J.C. came to work for her. One day she noticed that he was wearing one of her braided leather belts. She said, "J.C., kneel down." Then Mama said, "Repeat after me....'O my God I am heartily sorry for having offended you.'" She continued with the entire Act of Contrition and at the end said, "J.C., give me my belt." He said, "Yes Ma'am." J.C. stayed on for a long time. We called him the "butler."

My brother Charlie said, "Shouldn't we say the 'Our Father'?" And we did. Charlie left the room and Mama's breathing changed. I ran down the hall to get Charlie and when we got back she breathed her last peaceful breath. I know she heard all the stories and knew we were all there with her.

She wanted to be buried at sundown so that the Sandia Mountain would be ablaze in orange, red, and purple. The cemetery was just west of Sandia Mountain. After a personal wake service and funeral with lots more stories and mementos, we buried her as the sun was setting. It was cold that January 25, 1991. The Mariachi band from her favorite Mexican restaurant played "Resuscito" and all of Mama's favorite Spanish songs. Cousin Dot said, "Let's dance." We danced until dark throwing the flowers into the grave. It was like a Bergmann film.

My Retreat with Mama

During the summer of 1991 after Mama died, I wanted to make my eight-day retreat at Surfside Beach with Mama as my "director." I had kept all of her letters from 1954, when I went to Belgium for my novitiate, until January 1991. Her last card to me from Washington, D. C., was just a few days before she died.

I prepared for my special retreat by taking our family Cajun recipe book. I went to the fish market in Freeport and bought shrimp and crawfish. I also had a supply of okra, onions, bell peppers, celery, rice and tomatoes, so that I could fix the Cajun recipes Mama loved. I wanted to be immersed in her body and soul.

I started by reading her letters and putting them in chronological order. What a beautiful journey it was for me, seeing how through all the years, she had loved me, her firstborn, and supported me in all my endeavors. She was an excellent writer, giving brilliant descriptions of nature, especially during her retirement in Taos, New Mexico. She loved all God's creation and mirrored it in her descriptions of sunrises and sunsets, of the mountains and wildlife around her and of the plants and trees.

During that reading of her letters, I was inspired to write her story in first person, from the perspective of being the eleventh child. I wrote it from the bits and pieces I had gleaned from her and others. I let her be in me writing from her heart united with mine. I truly believe she was, writing these inspired words.

I believe that Mama, who bore me in her body, had a special part in my being re-created by the God events in my life. She continued her mother energy in my life as I prepared the crawfish etoufee' and made okra gumbo. I connected with her in the rising sun rippling on the waves, and in the immensity of the ocean, and in eating the wonderful Cajun food that she loved

A Miraculous Convergence

Mama was accomplished in convergences, like the one in which art friends in Lake Jackson invited me to go to Houston to an unusual workshop on "laughter." It was to be given by a nun who was a "wanna-be" stand-up comic. We drove to Houston and found her home, arriving early. Two elderly women were already there. After putting on our name tags, we sat down on a couch opposite these two darling women. One, who was particularly bright-eyed, said, "Oh! You're from Lake Jackson. My dearest friend, who died recently, has a daughter who is a nun in Lake Jackson. Her name is Josephine." I could feel my heart skip, and I said, "I am that nun." I could not imagine who she was and so I said, "And who are you?" She said, "I'm Cecilia Kelly." Wow, my brain started searching for its memories of her.

I had not seen Cecilia Kelly since 1943 when she was my confirmation god-mother. I had a flashback of her with flaming red hair and a big straw hat, and remembered her as Mama's best friend. I jumped up and hugged her. Needless to say, we hardly attended the workshop, but talked like school girls the whole time, telling the stories of 48 years. She had corresponded with Mama all those years.

Cecilia and her husband had been neighbors of Mama's brother, Charlie, in San Antonio. When Cecilia's husband was transferred by the railroad to Fort Worth, Charlie said, "You must look up my kid sister, Helen." That's how they met and became fast friends, talking on the phone every morning when their husbands had gone to work. Cecilia became a wise guide for Mama during some difficult times of raising a family. She was like an older sister that Mama needed.

During the workshop, we decided to get together on Mama's birthday, February 22, which was coming up shortly. I would bring all the photo albums and she'd make a birthday cake. We started a tradition of celebrating Mama's birthday each year until I left Lake Jackson.

At the first birthday party, Cecilia told me this priceless story. Mama had been frustrated about not being able to please Daddy. Cecilia suggested decorating the bathroom with plants and pretty towels and washcloths. Mama saved from her grocery money and purchased what she needed. She secretly decorated the one and only bathroom. After some prompting, Daddy noticed the changes and was very pleased. I'm sure that Cecilia was the confidante that Mama needed to express her feelings about Daddy.

I have often thought back on the miracle of meeting Cecilia and have relished the dove-tailing of each part of it. Had we not arrived early, I would probably have missed meeting Cecilia. Had my friends not invited me to go to this unusual "nun-thing," I would have missed out. If Cecilia had not gone to replace another person who couldn't go, she would not have been there. And all the way back to Uncle Charlie, if he had not mentioned "Look up my kid sister," Mama would never have met Cecilia. I was in touch with how the living and dead are all connected.

Because of the chance meeting with Cecilia, I was able to see Mama, as a young mother, through the eyes of her friend.

CHAPTER 13

THE WINDING JOURNEY FROM LAKE JACKSON TO TACOMA

In late 1992, I attended a wonderful Art Therapy course at the University of Houston in Clearlake. The drive there took about an hour each way. As I drove I listened to tapes about community living. The Art Therapy course gave me new counseling tools and insights into the subconscious, but the gift of going to Clearlake was what happened inside of me–a thirst to know more about community. One of the presenters on the tape was Vince Horan, former Beginning Experience International Board Member, who lived in Tacoma, Washington.

I phoned him to see if there would be a chance for me to come there to experience the kind of community he was talking about. He invited me to come for a visit in January of 1993, at which time he invited me to come and live with his family.

To move would mean to leave my beloved Lake Jackson. As I have described leaving people has always been excruciating for me. I was inspired to plan a blessed transition with a trip to Scotland and Ireland. Again, there was much synchronicity in all of this. The Beginning Experience Regional Conference for England, Scotland and Ireland was in Glasgow in August, 1993.

Adele owned the home in Lake Jackson where I lived. She was widowed and, in addition, had grieved the death of a daughter and a son. She was on the Houston team. We decided to go together to Glasgow for that Regional Conference. Then Adele would fly back to Houston and I would fly, not to Houston, but directly to Tacoma.

I had much to do to get ready for this trip. It would be my moving from Lake Jackson to Tacoma. Friends organized a garage sale and housecleaning. It was hot and damp that August day. The sale was a monetary success. I put the money toward the plane ticket. We left the next day for London and then on to Glasgow, a winding way to Tacoma.

One of the delights of the first day there was going to an ancient Spa and pool. What a way to let go of the tiredness and to get ready for the conference!

That evening we went to Saint Andrew's College, the venue for the conference. We were happy to be with all those wonderful people from Scotland, Northern Ireland, Ireland and England–all involved in this ministry. The conference got off to an excellent start with the traditional "parade of teams" with their beautifully decorated team banners. Many priests, nuns and the bishop attended.

For the skits, Adele and I had great fun doing "Bus Stop" which originated with Shirley Walden in 1979 on the Christchurch, New Zealand team. It presented a scene of two women at a Bus Stop sitting on a bench. One is a grand lady who is primping with lipstick, cosmetic brush, powder, rouge, mirror, comb and a nail file. She is reading a fashion magazine. The other woman is a tramp with a tousled wig, teeth missing (raisins), imitating the lady, taking stuff from her paper sack: roll-on deodorant, rough brush, cleanser, marks-a-lot, tin pan, wire brush, and carpenter's file. She is reading a comic book. A handsome gentleman comes by and walks off with the tramp.

The Conference workshops were excellent. The purpose of the regional conferences every other year is to keep local teams connected with one another and with the International Ministry Center in the United States and to provide on-going training and up-date. No number of letters or phone calls can give similar personal connection across the miles. Getting together under the same roof brings instant connection. These conferences are magic. Sparks of energy fly as friends from past conferences come together, recognize one another, hug and talk. For the "first-timers" it is a window into the vast beauty of the Beginning Experience family. In Glasgow I saw the lively exchange of ideas, information and feelings with people in this part of the world. There is no more significant way of preserving the thread that runs through the Beginning Experience other than the conventions and conferences. I saw first hand how these teams so far away respected and guarded the integrity of the process. They felt connected with each other and with the International Ministry Center in the United States.

On August 16, we left Saint Andrew's College early in the morning with the Derry team to start our journey to Northern Ireland. The ferry crossing was two and a half hours of sheer beauty, sunny all the way, and a great time for me to visit with the Derry Team. When we arrived in Northern Ireland, Hugh and Liam from Derry carried our luggage to the train bound for Belfast. We assumed that they would go directly to Derry, and to our surprise, when we got to our seats on the Belfast train, there they were. This was just so Irish. I can still see their smiles and the twinkle in their eyes as they said, "This is a dangerous place, you know. We couldn't leave you unescorted."

After two days with the Belfast team, seeing all the good they were doing, we went to Derry to stay with Bridie. She had prepared a feast of fresh Salmon. Her three daughters were there–beautiful Irish lasses who were step-dancers.

After dinner, Liam and Hugh drove us to the Carmelite Retreat Center where the Beginning Experience took place. On the drive there, we toured the war zones of Derry. Liam explained the centuries-long history of fighting between the English and the Irish. The oppression of the English and their cruelty to the peasant Irish led to their holding on to the northern part of Ireland. We got a glimpse of the devastation of this on-going war. I was even more awestruck that the Beginning Experience was flourishing in Ireland, where, at that time, divorce was not recognized by church or state and there was an on-going conflict between England and Ireland that is between the Protestants and the Catholics.

Once at the retreat center, we were greeted with a large group of Beginning Experience people who had come to hear me speak. I spoke of the personal power of Christ's suffering, death and resurrection lived in each one of the separated, divorced and widowed through the process of the Beginning Experience. I spoke of forgiveness and reconciliation. I was aware of the unique suffering of these people in Northern Ireland where the conflict between Protestants and Catholics had raged for years. This Beginning Experience team symbolized for me a special reconciliation because on it Protestants and Catholics worked together.

Next day, one of the team members took Adele and me on a grand tour of the north coast to *Giants Causeway*–thirty miles of basalt rock formation, thousands of hexagonal columns–standing in close formation. I sketched these and now carry this masterpiece of nature inside of me. (N)

That last evening in Derry, we went to an Irish pub. Two of Bridie's daughters were step-dancers. They were dressed in ornate green costumes and their feet and legs danced very fast. Nothing else moved except the smile on their faces and their bouncing hair. I loved this experience of Irish music and dancing at a local pub. (#32) The Irish play very hard.

From Derry, Northern Ireland, we went to Ireland. We drove along the coast of Donegal and then south along the Atlantic Ocean to Sligo. The trip was like a retreat, the four of us sharing our lives and spiritual journeys. We referred to this trip as "the journey to Emmaus" with the realization that as we talked, Jesus was revealing himself in the things we talked about and shared.

In Sligo, we experienced lovely Irish hospitality and the intense fervor of the West of Ireland Beginning Experience team. Fervor is an apt way to describe the Irish teams.

I was particularly touched by the story of one woman, plagued by guilt. Her husband had suffered a fatal heart attack right after she asked him to bring in the groceries. She suffered from "the if-onlys" that many people obsess about when they have lost a spouse. This woman let go of her guilt, closed the door on the past, and moved to new life.

The next day, we went to the mud flats to dig mussels. I was barefoot, up to mid-calf in squishy mud, plunging the "mussel-grabber" into the mud. Pulling my legs out, first one and then the other, without ending up sitting in the mud was quite a feat. We were successful in gathering a load of mussels for dinner that night.

The team chaplain took us to his "place of peace" where he goes to think and unwind. It is a niche in his "sitting room" in the Black Rocks overlooking the crashing waves of the Atlantic Ocean. I sketched the tide pools filled with little crustaceans and sea animals. (O) What an abundance of "exterior landscapes" that provided spiritual nourishment for the "interior landscapes" of the souls of the Irish team members!

On Sunday morning, we left on the bus to cross Ireland to Dublin where Dominic met and took us to eat Pub Grub. He gave us time to rest and then next day took us out to see the Dublin Lighthouse.

Sitting in a field of heather mixed with yellow wild flowers I sketched the lighthouse. The Irish Sea was on my left, with sun splashed sparkles on the water. The lighthouse was straight ahead. (P)

That evening, we met with the Dublin team in a lively exchange about the success of their team-effort to bring healing to the divorced and widowed in the Dublin area. We got to bed early, because Adele was leaving at 5:00 a.m. to return to Houston. It was the end of an era in my life and in hers. When I flew over the top of the world to Tacoma, Washington a new era began for me.

In Tacoma, I would be responding to Vince Horan's offer to come and live with them and be Nanny for their son, Jeremy, who was twelve. I could research community in the Puget Sound area which had many intentional communities. Like most of my other decisions to change locations or jobs this seemed to just fall into place, directed by God's providence and the synchronicity of the universe.

I had met with the Sisters of Saint Mary to present this plan and received their blessing. Again, I would be living in a family. Both Vince and his wife, Sandra, were counselors, specializing in family therapy. Learning from them would be an additional benefit.

CHAPTER 14

TACOMA WASHINGTON

As always the Holy Spirit directed my plans to go to Tacoma. I call this synchronicity. It just so happened that *Sojourners* magazine wrote a little clip about a worldwide convergence of intentional communities that would take place August 26-30, 1993, in Olympia, Washington. My plans, made before I saw this, were to arrive in Tacoma two days before this convergence and so I attended it.

The theme of the convention was "Celebration of Community" or "Sustainable Living Through Community." We stayed in university campus housing, attended the workshops in the main building and had delicious vegetarian meals served out of chuck wagons outside. The meal time and waiting in line provided great occasions for sharing. A straw-bale house was being constructed in the middle. The building process went on during the whole convention and at the end the house was completed.

In the plenary sessions and workshops, I saw the world as all connected. I felt great hope. We were given a world-wide vision of the future, the spiritual dimensions of community and plans for sustainability. On a very practical level, we learned about decision making, conflict resolution, and consensus, which was not only taught but experienced in our small groups. We learned to facilitate consensus, as well as to be part of the process. My head and heart were storing up abundance to share with both my religious community and with the Beginning Experience.

We experienced the famous Doctor Patch Adams, who energized us to live and work for the poor and forgotten. He shared his dream of free medical care which was later made into a film. Unlike Robin Williams, who aptly portrayed him, he was exceptionally tall. At the closing ceremony, he sent us off dancing.

We saw a presentation from the Eco-Village in Los Angeles where the Watts community, which had been burned out in the race riots, was retrofitted for housing and sustainable living. I met people from communities around the world: I talked to the people from Denmark where co-housing was very successful. I met the founders of Findhorn, Scotland, where the foundations of community were laid on their rocky northern coast. I spoke with the founder of the Alpha Farm in Oregon who told of the painful learning experiences of coming to unity in diversity. That meant that each side had to let go of some treasured ideas and, out of compassion for the whole, come to unity of purpose, not identical thinking. At the Alpha Farm, that process was consensus, not voting which makes the majority rule, but by calmly discussing differences and coming to agreement on what each side could accept.

As I was deciding to go to Tacoma and research community, my main attraction was the number of intentional communities that were located in the Puget Sound area and in Oregon. However, that convention brought together people from all over the world. My project of writing about community got a huge jump start here. I simply took all my notes, tapes, and literature from this convention and began compiling my resource book on community.

After that memorable convention, I settled into living with the Horans. Both Vince and Sandra had been married before and had experienced failure in marriage. They had each made the Beginning Experience and had let go of the past, the mistakes and the pain of their former marriages. They had been healed and transformed into two people who could love themselves and each other and this family.

Sandra had two children, Bridget who lived in an apartment and worked, and Jayson who was in high school and lived at home. Vince brought no children into this marriage, but he and Sandra had Jeremy together. Vince was overjoyed at his first-born.

In their blended family, it was evident they had forged a loving atmosphere through pain and hard work. It didn't just happen. I considered them to be a model for blended families. They truly lived out The Vision of the Beginning Experience, "people transformed and free again to love."

The source of life in this home was positive energy. I felt immediately the absence of shaming and criticism. Instead, I felt the presence of unconditional love and acceptance. The love and affection between Vince and Sandra radiate to the others and created ease in giving hugs and saying "I love you" spontaneously and often, in the safety of this house. Everyone felt safe being themselves regardless of their dark or light moods.

Vince and Sandra had learned and then put into practice, unconditional love of each other and the kids. There were no surprises or inconsistencies.

Before going there, I thought I knew what unconditional love and acceptance was. But there I saw demonstrated, daily and consistently, a loving of each one that was neither based on how well one performed nor the behavior, attitude, personality, or anything about another person. Vince and Sandra did not try to control their children thus leaving them free to learn life's lessons. Their motivation in being parents was not for their sons and daughter to live up to their expectations but to be the best of who they were. They shared their wisdom with the kids and then left the decision up to them. They exercised great self discipline by doing that. They did not interrupt the process by inserting a self serving focus. Because they had consistently done this all along, it worked. Their children were self motivated to make necessary changes, eventually, and to be responsible for themselves.

For example, Jayson had just opened his own checking account at the bank. He worked part-time after school and, from his salary he was responsible for the insurance, gasoline and upkeep of his car, as well as his long distance telephone calls and recreation. Vince and Sandra offered to teach him how to balance his check book and to budget so that he would have enough money to pay the big bills when they came due. He chose not to ask for their help. Vince and Sandra's attitude was always of sharing their wisdom and opinions and then letting go. I never heard them raise their voices. They always calmly offered information and then they let go. There were never any threats. There was great trust and respect.

Each member of the family was free to express all feelings. That of course did not give anyone license to cause harm to oneself or another or to destroy material things of value.

Each one paid attention to the feelings of others, listened to those feelings, and honored them, but did not take responsibility for them. There was no fear of expressing needs in that family. Needs for safety, security, love, affection, all bodily, spiritual and emotional needs

103

were honored and listened to and responded to. As far as I could tell, no one here felt discounted. They all knew that they could feel their feelings, speak their needs, be heard and have their needs met. They recognized the fact that feelings represent what is going on at the deepest level and that in honoring feelings and needs they honored the person.

Jeremy, for example, had been feeling left out by Bridget and Jayson who were older and had the same biological parents. He sometimes annoyed Jayson with attention-getting and obnoxious behavior. At a family meeting, Jayson asked Jeremy to stop that behavior and at that point, Jeremy got in touch with his deep sadness at being left out. At the family meeting, the two boys agreed to spend more time together each week.

A vital part of this family was taking responsibility and being accountable. Each one agreed to care for and love oneself, and others and God's material world. If, either intentionally or unintentionally, someone broke this agreement then there was no shaming, punishing, or fear-producing outburst to bring about compliance. Instead there was a simple tool used, which all in this family had done many times. And which I did too. It was the "Think Paper." It was very simple. It consisted in answering three questions in writing.

1. What happened? What was going on inside of me at that time?
2. How will I repair the damage or make amends?
3. How will I avoid this happening in the future?

Then it was shared with the people involved. There was never need for punishment or for further focus on the negative behavior. This meant that there was no shame or hopeless or helpless feelings and no unrealistic guilt.

Certainly, there were times when Vince and Sandra needed to point out behavior or to correct. This was done gently, with a loving tone of voice and the content of the correction was clear.

One of the biggest contributors to the positive energy in this home was the ability to play and have fun. Recreation was truly recreation here. What struck me was unplanned play–inserting play into every nook and cranny of the day. If there was even a small segment of time–say an hour–someone might say, "Let's get in the boat and go water skiing." (They lived on a lake.) Another favorite was just hanging out.

The boys had weekly chores: dishes, laundry, and cleaning. They received an allowance.

Living in this family was a loving, joyful and healing experience for me. I learned how family members cherish one another.

I felt close to Jeremy. That year I was able to see the world through the eyes and heart of a 12 year old boy. I learned to enjoy his movies and music and just being with him. And I taught him a lot about geography, history and relating to older people.

I could recount many stories, but one will suffice. I picked him up from school every day and he would turn the radio dial to his favorite station. One day, he chose music of the 60's and said, "This is my favorite, 'oldies.'" I was imagining the 20's as 'oldies' and said, "That's not 'oldies,'" to which he replied: "For you, Josephine, 'new releases.'"

Every day after school, we went to McDonald's and he got "Two For": two hamburgers and two French fries and a coke for $2.00. Never mind that at 6:30 he would eat a full dinner.

The house rang with laughter and energy each morning and after school. It was smooth. Many friends frequented the Horans.

Vince and Sandra were both "graduates" of the Beginning Experience and demonstrated what they had gained by moving far beyond their initial "beginning." They were a marvelous example of the fruition of *The Vision of the Beginning Experience*, which is "a hurting people healed, transformed and free again to love themselves, others and God." I was grateful to see and be immersed in the "rest of the story."

Even when not fully achievable, I considered the Horan family a model to strive for.

CHAPTER 15

MY L'ARCHE EXPERIENCE

Living in L'Arche and the Beginning Experience were the peak moments of my life. I saw living in L'Arche, as a service, a completion of what was begun in me by the invitation to reach out, given at the end of the Beginning Experience. I did not plan or contrive either of these. I could never have dreamed them up. They were God's grace in my life.

L'Arche, French for "the Ark," referring to Noah's ark, a refuge for all God's creatures, was founded as an international network of local communities providing home for developmentally disabled adults.

I first encountered L'Arche in 1983 when I worked at Saint Theresa's Home in Fort Worth. I had facilitated a support group of young volunteer women who worked with children with emotional problems. I used *Community and Growth*, by Jean Vanier as a resource for our weekly discussions, applying his wisdom to living in community. Thus, I experienced L'Arche vicariously. I said to myself, "Someday I may find one of those communities to visit."

Ten years later I moved to Tacoma to study intentional communities, to write a resource book for living in community, and to work for the Horans by being nanny to Jeremy.

Soon after I arrived in Tacoma, I signed up for a workshop on Vashon Island and was given a ride there by a woman who told me of her friend's involvement with a community called L'Arche. Yes, that was the same L'Arche that I had read about ten years earlier. I could hardly believe that there was a L'Arche here in Tacoma. My mind was racing. How could I incorporate this L'Arche into my study of intentional communities?

It took several months to get up the courage to approach meeting L'Arche "in the flesh." I called and was told about a monthly gathering of L'Arche folks with visitors. So I went. The meeting was in the large living room of The Farmhouse. I do not recall any of the details, but

I remember the laughter, loving kindness, hospitality and the feeling of being home. After I returned for the second monthly gathering, I approached someone about becoming a volunteer at L'Arche.

As a volunteer I cooked supper every Monday at Esperanza where five core members (residents) lived with their assistants (staff). I learned a great deal about going with the flow: letting the evening unfold with baths going on, with card games in the living room, with visitors dropping by and sharing their lives, and watching sports events on TV. All was about taking time with each other.

I met Sister Madeleine, a Dominican sister who had worked in L'Arche for a long time. I observed her calm way and genuine love for all. She taught me the L'Arche way in her simplicity and humility. I admit, when I first went, I had a "top sergeant" mentality. I wanted everything to be scheduled and to come off just the way I expected. I learned quickly that going with the flow is easier than forcing my will. That first encounter with L'Arche was transformational for me. Just being in that home once a week "gentled" my forceful attitude.

I learned that besides Esperanza and The Farmhouse there were other homes in the L'Arche community: Hilltop, Hopespring (the House of Prayer), Anawim, and soon-to be-opened Ananda, the children's home.

The next significant encounter with L'Arche was on Good Friday 1994 at the Stations of the Cross. The whole community gathered in the open air barn of Ananda for the enactment by the core members of the stations. I had never seen Bill Downey. He was Jesus in the scene of the Condemnation. He was dressed in his suit and tie and British style hat. Over all this was a scarlet satin cloak. Each station was a still life with all the core members involved. I was moved to tears by each re-enactment and by the simple, direct script that was read.

Not long after that touching encounter, there was an open house at Ananda, the Children's Home that was opening. That was a L'Arche dream fulfilled with the coming of Bobby, the first child. The Sanskrit name Ananda means "The joy without which the world would cease to exist." I meditated on those words for a long time and applied them to other virtues, such as "The peace without which....The love without which...The patience without which..."and on and on. Repeating these phrases and putting myself into them gave me energy to strive for love and peace and patience because our weary world depended on it.

L'Arche was fast becoming a wonderful world for me. I had a sense there of cooperation, unconditional love, acceptance, hospitality, openness. I wanted to be part of that world.

I drove by Hilltop House but was afraid to knock on the door. I saw Bill sitting in the window–suit, tie, hat and all. I felt like a child tiptoeing around not to be heard. Later, when I decided to work at L'Arche, I was assigned to Hilltop House and Bill became the one I accompanied.

I re-read *Community and Growth*, about L'Arche, as a community dedicated to people with developmental disabilities. I knew how far I was from living this ideal, but I wanted to be immersed in it and most of all I wanted to break through my fear of people with developmental disabilities and to live with them. I decided, when my commitment as Nanny for Jeremy ended, I would ask to work as an assistant at L'Arche.

The first day I lived at Hilltop I began to see that L'Arche was about relationships, not about a job to be done. I sat at the desk in my room and read a poster about what people with mental handicaps can do. I do not recall each gift, but they were all of the heart, like dancing, being spontaneous, laughing for no reason at all, living in the present moment, being grateful, giving hugs, being creative, being loyal and most of all, loving unconditionally. I sat there and prayed that God would take away my fears.

I learned very soon that living and working in L'Arche meant not taking care of those "poor disabled people." I learned not to ever do for them what they could do by themselves: not crippling or disabling them further and, most of all, not feeling sorry for them, all of which puts the focus on me and my control. The response was always to *"be with."* That very first day, my seeing changed and my fears began to recede. *"Being with"* was not difficult, after all.

Being with Bill, Dick, Wally, Mark and Les became comfortable. I was the only woman at Hilltop. All the core members and assistants were men. Sports was a big item for them. Monday night football and Saturday afternoon college games were always on the agenda.

The living room was a long room with a television at one end. I enjoyed football but needed something to do while we watched.

I found a table and installed it at the opposite end of the room. I put a sewing machine on top and put a basket out for items to be mended. The basket soon filled with blue jeans, shirts, underwear and then dish towels and bath towels. Items from the other houses also came in. So I was happy being with the guys watching the games. I could follow along while sewing and I could cheer especially for the Dallas Cowboys and Notre Dame.

It was easy to love these guys. Wally was the oldest. He literally danced through life, bearing the nickname of "Mr. Twinkle Toes." Every afternoon, when he came home, he played "Crazy Eights." He had an electric card shuffler which loudly signaled "Let's begin." Several of us would gather, only to be beaten by Wally–the pro. Despite his own health problems he was always concerned about others. He wrote lots of letters, giving uplifting messages to those who were feeling bad. But most of all he was Irish to the core and sang the traditional Irish songs. His room was decorated for the Leprechaun he was.

Mark, the youngest, arrived soon after me. He was tall and handsome and dressed impeccably. He worked at the YMCA folding towels and giving cheer to all he met there. One of my duties was to assist him with his bath. I especially enjoyed washing his hair, knowing how great I felt to have someone massage my head. He was grateful for everything I did. His room was filled with his favorite sports heroes. He was an expert on sports statistics and information.

Les was the entertainer. He did a marvelous Elvis act and was Santa Claus every Christmas. We stored the costumes in the basement, but occasionally they would be "stolen" and a spontaneous Elvis act would take place. He was a loyal farm worker. Because he was strong, he did big jobs at the Farm and Gardens. He and Dick helped the staff in building the large greenhouse. The greenhouse "kit" was ordered and the hard plastic panels and metal structure were put together, and out came an incredible huge greenhouse.

Dick was the other farm worker at Hilltop. He was artistic, with a keen sense of color and design. Every morning, before going to work, he would color intricate pictures in coloring books. He had a supply of felt pens which he kept in a large cherry crate. He sat at the head of the dining room table and concentrated on coloring the design before him. Then, after work and his shower and, again, before going to bed, he methodically did his art.

I learned a big lesson from Dick. Every year L'Arche had an auction for the benefit of Ananda house and the children. I asked Dick if I could take one of his "paintings" to get it matted and framed to sell at the auction. He said, "I threw them all away." I was aghast. How could he have thrown away those beautiful works of art? An assistant said, "Josephine, you don't understand; for Dick the only thing that's important is the doing of the painting." I asked Dick to please do another one for the auction. It brought in $300. But the victory was what Dick taught me: to focus on the journey, not the destination, to focus on doing art, not on judging the product.

Bill was my special responsibility. His parents had come over to Tacoma from Donegal, Ireland. He inherited a heart of gold and a will to go with it. I had a hard time understanding his speech at first, so I wrote down the words he said and gradually learned his large vocabulary. He had a lovely way of saying my name when he wasn't saying, "Oh, Ma-Ma." He was all heart. Others of us are big on thinking, analyzing and evaluating. For Bill, his heart led all. He accepted me just as I was. (#s 29 and 30)

He got into a few tiffs with Dick because he egged Dick on. He'd get into Dick's bed, fully clothed and refuse to move. So Dick got him back by hiding his Bible. Since Bill would not go to church without his Bible–and his keys, and his church envelope, and his shoe horn, and his wallet–we were late for church one Sunday. I finally found Bill's Bible on the top shelf in Dick's room, where Dick said that Bill (4'9"tall) had put it. I just laughed about it and asked Dick not to do that again.

After Mass we'd often go to Denny's for the "Grand Slam" breakfast. Each one had his wallet and some dollar bills for tips. One Sunday, Bill put a $50 bill on the table. We never found out where he'd gotten it.

Bill loved to greet everyone in Denny's or in McDonald's-- especially the children. My favorite excursion with Bill was to ride the Vashon Island ferry back and forth in the afternoon when the children were getting out of school in Tacoma. Bill, in his wheelchair, would shake hands with each child. His smile and merry eyes connected with them. He was a great connector.

We all attended Saint Leo's, the Jesuit church downtown. I often sat in the front row with our deaf core members to experience the dramatic "sign-ing" of the readings and songs. Our core members often danced in the aisles–discreetly, of course.

Every L'Arche throughout the world had a special work to provide meaningful employment for the people who lived at L'Arche. For our L'Arche, the work was the Farm and Gardens. Several acres next to the Farmhouse were planted in flowers. The core members planted the seeds in tiny seedling containers and tended them in the greenhouses. Sometimes, we all helped with transplanting the seedlings to larger containers. Finally, when the frost was over, the seedling flowers were planted in rows according to variety and color. We all helped with the planting and it was fun, especially since there were cool breezes and no hot Texas sun. We sang, played and planted under the supervision of those who ran the farm.

At harvest, the harvesters would sleep in tents near the fields and get up at 4:00 a.m. just before sunrise and cut the flowers, putting them in large buckets according to kind and color. That day we would all gather to create the bundles of cut flowers that went to the markets for sale. I loved going from container to container picking out just the right combination of flowers, rubber banding them together and cutting off the straggly stems. The flowers that were grown to be dried were bundled and hung upside down from the barn rafters, waiting to be made into wreaths for the holidays.

Abundance was the theme song. It was the "ocean" in which we all lived. There were many helps and safeguards for living in God's abundance. Foremost, were the five "Rules of Cooperation": no scarcity, no secrets, no power plays, equal rights and no rescues. Every morning we had a staff house meeting based on the "Rules of Cooperation" and on communicating well. There was a great attempt not to live in confusion. Everyone knew what was expected and we all aimed at cooperating, so that each one carried some of the load.

The spiritual benefits were also abundant. Each Advent and Lent, we went to the Trappist Monastery–Guadalupe–in Oregon for retreat. Half of the community went in Advent and the other half went in Lent. The retreat coordinators decided on a theme and a schedule which involved the monks giving talks and the core members doing skits or art work to apply the talk. We also went to hear the monks, dressed in their long white robes, sing the beautiful melodies of the Divine Office.

The monastery was very modern with lovely guest houses. I was always with Bill. I had the honor of taking part in his joy at each monk's talk and I listened to him talk about his friendship with them. Brother Mark was his favorite. At night, I did the same bedtime routines as when we were at home. I slept on the floor near him to help him to the bathroom and to try to get him back to sleep. That was always a challenge. He just had more energy than all of us.

Another special journey was to the Swinomish—the Native American Long House people. The tribe had come to the area 10,000 years earlier, that would be long before Abraham. They built long houses for their community life. Every year they invited us to come to their Spirituality Center. They spoke to us of their "way" of peace, living in harmony with the earth, water, salmon and all of nature. At the conclusion of our visit, they gave us gifts—blankets, jewelry, pottery, baskets. Gift-giving is the tradition of abundance of the Native American peoples.

All the assistants went each year to a special L'Arche retreat with other L'Arche members from around the world. I went one year to Canada, to Alberta and another year to Quebec. The retreats were conducted by leaders in L'Arche International.

I received in-depth understanding of abundance—the foundation of L'Arche. Most of all, I was happy to be with the young assistants who had given themselves to this ministry. Like me they were learning the special spirituality of L'Arche—that each person, disabled or not, has a unique and mysterious value. I began to see L'Arche as a "boot camp" for life. For the young assistants who came for a few years before going on to other careers, it was a strong foundation for a dedicated life.

I often spent my day away in the library at Hopespring surrounded by the forest, watching the seasons: the budding and fruiting and especially the snowing. That was where I continued my serious journaling to and from God. I wanted to hear what God was saying to me in all the events and people in my life at L'Arche. I went often to the little chapel at Hopespring and just sat on the floor in front of the Blessed Sacrament. I was just "be-ing," not doing.

Not long after I arrived, Sister Christella, the L'Arche pastor, offered to direct a retreat for me. (#31) Each day had a simple theme. The first day was, "I know God loves me, I am not afraid." I painted a robin's nest with eggs to symbolize the theme. These words and that painting have become a wellspring inside my heart giving me peace and safety.

Another day the theme was, "I am the Vine. You are the branches." I painted the vine in the form of a cross with prominent roots down into the earth. It represented to me that Christ is rooted in the soil of our humanity.

Living day to day in community with Bill, Les, Wally, Dick and Mark, all people who were not "blessed" with what our world calls "gifted-ness," gave me a deep appreciation of their abundance. They never tried to be what they were not. They spoke and acted from the heart. They were open to the present moment, to what was going on right then. People were most important. Friendship was paramount. They were not perfect. Working out relationships was the only focus–not who's right or who's better.

Every year on Palm Sunday, we had a reconciliation rite. It con-sisted of telling a Jesus story with all participating in the dramatiza-tion. After the story each was given a two-sided sign. One side said "Thank you" and the other side said "I'm sorry." Each wore the sign and then went to each person and said, "Thank you for..." and "I'm sorry for..." This was one of the easiest and most direct reconciliations that I'd ever experienced.

Some core members who came to L'Arche had deep wounds from being abandoned or from having been treated violently. So for me and all of the assistants we had to learn to be loving and patient. We were being taught the most basic foundation of love: to see God in others. Learning patience brought out in me my most negative char-acter defect of trying to control. I learned that in letting go, God al-ways gave me what I needed in each difficult situation.

Before working at L'Arche, I swore I would never "diaper" an adult man. During the last year of Bill's life, I changed his Depends Undergarments at least six times a day. I did it with real joy. God gave me that free gift.

I often slept in the room with him and got up several times at night. I had a lot of interrupted sleep. The miracle of it–direct from God–was that I always got up with joy to care for someone I loved. I put forth no effort, nor was that difficult to do.

One night shortly before Bill died, I was sleeping on the little bed near him and I was awakened by the smell of a bowel movement.

He was still asleep, so I went down to the laundry and got some old cloths, a plastic bag and a bucket of warm water and went back. When he awoke, he said, "It stinks!" I cleaned up the mess and washed him with the warm water and changed the bed. After we finished I sat on the bed next to him and he said, "Oh, Ma-Ma. I love you." Such love in both of us.

Soon, after that night, I went to the Beginning Experience Board Meeting in Detroit. I told the board members of the miracle of acceptance and joy that God had given me in caring for Bill. I likened it to the joy a mother feels despite interrupted sleep and dirty diapers. And since I was not, and never would be a mother, I knew Bill was the gift/miracle of my life.

I stayed an extra day in Detroit to rest up before returning to L'Arche. I phoned to tell Bill that I'd be home at 3:00 p.m. the next day. He died about 1:00 p.m., so I wasn't there with him. When I got there, I went into his room, where he was laid out, fully dressed in suit and tie, surrounded by burning candles and I had a little talk with him. I'll admit I fussed at him for leaving before I got back. Then I reached down to touch his knee, which often slipped out of joint. I would always massage it back in place. And it was out of joint. I did at that moment suffer the "what ifs:" "I'd not spent an extra day in Detroit...I'd have massaged his knee back in place...Or I'd have been with him." I started my grieving for him then. I wrote to and from him. He answered me in his voice with the intonations and crescendos that punctuated his sentences.

L'Arche's gift to me was a certitude of abundance in the midst of weakness. My belief that God does for us and in us what we cannot do for ourselves was reinforced. Thank you L'Arche. Thank you God.

CHAPTER 16

ANOTHER WINDING JOURNEY FROM TACOMA TO WICHITA FALLS

After Bill died, I sensed that my time at L'Arche was coming to an end. I began writing to and from God about this feeling. One day I wrote, Wichita Falls in my journal. I had never thought about Wichita Falls. I called Sister Devota in Wichita Falls and asked her about coming there. She was delighted and we talked about a House of Prayer of which both of us had been dreaming.

In order to ease the pain of leaving L'Arche, I planned a transition trip which materialized into an Inside Passage Ferry Cruise to Alaska.

I said goodbye to all in L'Arche. A friend, a L'Arche assistant from Poland, and I took the bus to Bellingham, Washington, to board the Alaska Highway Ferry. The first evening and night we went between mainland Canada on the east and Vancouver Island on the west. We passed among many islands.

The sun came up about 2:30 a.m. We got up at 4:00 to watch the whales and got wet and cold on the deck. The only choppy part of the trip was when we were on the open ocean from Port Hardy to our first stop in Ketchikan–the place of Native American Totems. First my friends and I found a church and went to Mass. The pastor introduced all the visitors. He was interested that we were from L'Arche. I talked also about Beginning Experience, which they knew about since there was a group in Anchorage. We visited after Mass at coffee and donuts and, since it was pouring rain, got a ride to the museum which was an excellent orientation to Alaska and Native American culture.

Once in Juneau, before checking into the motel, we went to the booking office to get tickets for boat tours. We signed up for a day long boat tour to see the glaciers. We got close to them and saw and heard the "calving off" when a huge iceberg broke off and crashed into the water.

The most exciting, though, was the raft trip on the river next to the Mendenhall Glacier at Juneau. We wore cozy life vests and helped row the inflated raft along the river and through mild rapids. I felt dangerously close to nature with the huge ice glacier above us and the fast moving river under us. I physically broke through my fear and my body relaxed.

For Native Americans, all of nature is symbolic of the spirit life. A beautiful mural in Juneau depicted the Native American account of the creation of the world. The Raven was the symbol of wisdom and the Bear represented strength.

Our motel was next to a Native American museum. I spent every spare hour in that living history. The Aleuts were seafaring and made their boats from the whale's skin and bones. They made their clothing and got their food from the whales. My favorite piece in the museum was a beautifully carved little cup which was used to give the whale a drink before they killed it. They had such respect for life and only killed in order to survive. They depended totally on whales and considered them sacred.

I carry the Raven, the Bear, the Eagle, the Whale in my heart, as well as the spirituality of these people who came to what would become Alaska. They crossed the Bering Strait probably 20,000 years before. I am always fascinated by the migrations of people. Just thinking of their courage and steadfastness helped put my grief on leaving L'Arche in perspective.

After our days in Juneau, we said goodbye. My friends returned to Tacoma and I flew to Fairbanks to be with the Beginning Experience team. From Fairbanks I was taken up through Denali Park on a bus tour where we could see Danali (Mount McKinley, highest peak in North America) clearly. The serpentine river at its base and the colors in its crevices were unusually beautiful. That evening I painted a composite of this experience, but I found it impossible to express the vastness of this river and The Mountain.

In Fairbanks, I had a marvelous time sharing with and listening to the Beginning Experience team. Participants came from as far north as Barrow on the Arctic Ocean. The labor of taking this ministry to the far reaches of Alaska was awesome. This team circled out from Fairbanks to reach those in remote places who needed its healing ministry. My heart was singing, knowing that the Beginning Experience was alive and was truly helping many in the far north.

Father Tim Sanders, who had been the faithful Beginning Experience chaplain for many years, took me along the famous oil pipeline and up to Saint Rafael's Church where he said Mass on weekends. The parishioners had built that church with their own hands. The pastor there was a sturdy Native American woman.

All too soon, my time to leave Alaska came to an end and I boarded the plane for Dallas/Fort Worth. I journaled on the plane, trying to think and feel what world I was leaving and what world I was entering. My heart, still full of L'Arche, made room to include Native Americans, Ravens and Bears, the Beginning Experience in Alaska, the love of friends, and God's infinite love and presence in and through all. On June 8, I left Alaska's freezing night temperatures and went to Wichita Falls for the hottest summer (108°) in years.

CHAPTER 17

WICHITA FALLS

Along with the high temperatures, I was warmly welcomed by Sister Devota, who was a native of Wichita Falls. The first night we watched the local news. The weather report was named "Storm Team Command Center." I was shocked. I'd never heard of such a thing. The weather report was warning of tornados in the area. The Wichita Falls tornado of 1979 had destroyed about 5,000 homes, one of which was Sister Devota's sister's home. Sister Devota took out her little black weather box radio and the map giving county lines. She explained that the safest place in the house was her inside bathroom. The storm eventually passed, but I kept wondering why God had told me to go there.

In searching for a thrift store one day, we stumbled upon the First Step Family Store. We saw a hexagon shaped glass top table with four cane back chairs for $100. More important than this purchase was my discovery that First Step was the women's shelter in Wichita Falls. I became interested in volunteering there.

I soon attended the volunteer training. The Volunteer Coordinator was a soft- spoken, competent and caring woman. In the course I learned about the traps and difficulties that abused women experience. Almost all the staff at First Step knew of abuse first hand. I was assigned to help with the Thursday night counseling group. The woman who led it emphasized the support and self-determination needed to overcome the pitfall of returning to an abusive situation. I was grateful to be a part of their support in avoiding entrapment in abuse. Many of these women took hold of their lives.

Years later I'd run into one of them and hear the rest of the story. There were many stories of finishing school, living successfully on their own, of working in jobs they loved. When I was helping in the Thursday night group I often did meditations with them, envisioning healing and hope. Each time I ran into one of them they spoke of those meditations.

An inspiration from God was my desire to provide Beginning Experience in Wichita Falls. My first counseling client was divorced. In addition two priests with long connections to Beginning Experience served in the area and were enthusiastic about introducing the program there.

I arranged to take that first client to Fort Worth for the August 1998 weekend. I cooked for the group. My client found release from her pain and found new life. She was grateful to have gone and was committed to helping in Wichita Falls.

The Dallas/Fort Worth Beginning Experience team agreed to go and conduct the weekend in Wichita Falls. We held it right in our House of Prayer. We split the beds with one sleeping on the box springs and the other on the mattress on the floor. Our house was bulging at the seams with more than 20 people. It was cozy.

Those who came as the first Wichita Falls participants were visibly transformed by the process. Dear Sister Devota offered to coordinate the kitchen and so she was present for the entire weekend. Afterwards she spoke passionately of the obvious transformation that she had witnessed. She had heard all the talks and marveled at their depth. She was touched by the stories. She saw, unfolding before her eyes, a spectacular change in each participant. She described the faces of those who came in the door on Friday night as depressed and down-cast and when they left on Sunday as smiling, and bright-eyed. She summed it up by exclaiming, "I saw resurrection on that weekend."

I was happy that, as an outsider, Sister Devota had seen the extent of peace and joy given by the Beginning Experience. She became an enthusiastic "cheer-leader" for our having the weekends at our home, so together we hosted them for many years.

Soon after my arrival, Sister Devota and I drove to Albuquerque to visit my father. The highlight of our time with him was a picnic. I would have just gone to buy Subway sandwiches and drinks, but no. I had forgotten that when I was a child all picnics were "from scratch." So we went with Daddy to the supermarket and bought "from scratch" everything for the picnic then headed toward Sandia Mountain. We found the right spot. It was dangerously rough terrain. (#33) We had to go down rock steps to get to the table. I was a bit nervous each time Daddy moved, but he had a wonderful time. He never forgot that picnic and even when his memory diminished he referred to "our picnic."

After leaving Albuquerque, Sister Devota and I drove up to Santa Fe and then along the Rio Grande River–the path of the conquistadors–to Taos. Holy Cross Hospital in Taos had been staffed by the Holy Family of Nazareth Sisters. Sister Devota whose sister had been stationed there was keen on seeing it. We found it but it was no longer a hospital. Daddy had been on the Board of Trustees for the hospital and had been responsible for the first ambulance service up to Taos Ski Valley. That trip brought back happy memories of how active and community-minded my parents had been during their 18 years in Taos.

I wanted to drive out to see my parent's house. I remembered the way and we found it. It looked the same from the outside. No one was home, so we peered through the windows into the big room. The furniture seemed very foreign–light in color–and it made a difference in the "feel" of the house which had been my second home. I had watched from the time its adobes were made right there on the property from mud and straw, to the installing of the windows and doors brought from Dallas, to the commissioning of the Santa Fe "Santo" carver who carved the Indian bread woman into the wonderful wood that became the front door, to the hand blown glass light fixtures and wrought iron from Mexico. The house was a collection which Mama and Daddy had accumulated and carried from Dallas to Taos in Daddy's Scout with Mama sitting in the back holding it all together.

That home somehow embodied their spirits even though they no longer lived there. Its name was "Casa -30-." Daddy being a newspaperman had named it the way all journalism stories end: -30-.

We were grateful to have taken this trip to really visit Daddy before he began to slow down. We happily arrived back in Wichita Falls. In addition to counseling, volunteering at First Step with the abused women, and getting a Beginning Experience team trained and presenting two weekends a year, I saw a need to console people experiencing grief during the holidays. I created a program, "Hope for the Holidays," designed for those saddened by the loss of a loved one and who were dreading the holidays. The weekly sessions ran from before Thanksgiving through Christmas and New Years. The program not only gave valuable information unique to holiday grieving but also gave the participants close support from one another other. The sharing of their pain significantly helped lighten the load, giving them hope.

Sister Patricia Ridgley and Linda Hajek gave us a unique gift. They planted a native garden for us. It was located just outside our newly created enclosed porch. It had a serpentine shaped border sectioning off the southwest inside corner of the house. A tree had been cut down from that corner and had left dangerously uneven ground. The garden was a perfect solution to the problem.

In the distance, behind the garden, was the statue of the Sacred Heart which had been at the Academy of Mary Immaculate from the time it was built in 1904. Our house was the convent for the new diocesan school which replaced the academy. That wonderful statue came to it.

So Patty and Linda came in a pickup filled with native plants from their Dallas garden and planted them for us. They brought manure to enrich the soil. The plants were very healthy after their first season.

Right before the start of the Iraq war in 2003, I joined a group that was forming. We called ourselves *The Wichita Falls Peace and Freedom Coalition.* The group was initially quite large. We organized a demonstration to protest the war that was coming. It was awfully cold that day, but many people joined us. We received good coverage in our local newspaper and on our local television stations.

In addition to this peace group, I was intent on having a group that would pray for peace and so the "Interfaith Peace Prayer Group" started. We began with a prayer that put us in solidarity with the women of Baghdad who were praying for peace at the Orthodox Church–old Saint Mary's Church. We discovered that Our Lady is prominent in the Qur'an. My friend Mahbooba, who is Muslim from Afghanistan, joined us. We met every Sunday evening starting in March of 2003. The Holy Spirit inspired each prayer time.

We experienced Tibetan Buddhist prayer practices, Hindu chanting for peace, films, lectures, news articles, music, poetry, Native American spirituality, Golden Bowls, Celtic spirituality, planting seeds, drumming, singing for peace using "Make Me a Channel of Your Peace." Whatever the Spirit sent us, we embraced. We created our "Peace Tree" with blue streamers of peace prayers, origami white doves, red jasmine blooms of hope and butterflies of resurrection.

That weekly experience has been one of the dearest of my life. We held candlelight vigils honoring our fallen dead and tolled bells for those who shed their blood. The "Interfaith Peace Prayer Group" provided a meaningful way of actually living non-violence and supporting one another in working for peace.

For years, my arthritic knees caused me a lot of pain. I tried everything to avoid having knee replacement surgery. To relieve the pain and to avoid excessive amounts of pain medication, I practiced the Buddhist meditation called *Tonglen*. It is quite simple. While breathing *in* you accept the pain and when you breathe *out* you connect with and send out compassion to a person or group of people who are suffering something similar. I connected with the children in the war zones and in Africa who were amputees. I had photos of those children around my room and in my daybook. I started each day using *Tonglen and* then practiced it when I was in pain.

The effect was spiritual. In using *Tonglen,* I bore the pain longer than I normally would have. Eventually I had the right knee replacement in 2006 and the next year I had the left one replaced.

Being immobilized during the surgery and the days after, rendered me helpless and dependent on the care of others. In this letting go, I lived the process of the Beginning Experience. I entered into my own suffering and dying and came to resurrection in union with Christ. Abundance came to me in the resulting mobility and freedom from pain that I found.

Today that abundance is multiplied when I sit in the garden planted by Sister Patricia Ridgley and Linda Hajek. Plants bloom both in spring and fall. Purple iris is the first to bloom during Lent, and then the yellow iris comes out during Easter. This happens every year on schedule. Summer bloomers come next. Mexican petunias (Ruellia) are prolific and have even burrowed under the cement slab at the door. Their lavender blooms hide in the dark green foliage. Catnip oozes over and around all empty spaces. Coreopsis remains hardy with its golden blooms lasting all summer. Artemesia also takes over, spreading its dusty leaves everywhere. In the autumn the tiny white asters come out.

Hummingbirds come to the feeders and birds come to the bird-bath as Saint Francis looks out over all. Every year I plant a new crop of zinnias from the harvested seed to add life and color. This array of gentle color and vegetation has become the "Peace Garden." It gives me a great deal of serenity as I sit in it, just letting God love me in the breeze.

CHAPTER 18

DADDY
Wylie Stewart

Although Mama and her family had a great influence on me, I believe that Daddy's life and my relationship with him had a more far-reaching influence on the creation of the Beginning Experience.

My first encounter with Daddy was when he saw me soon after I was born. I was told that he cried. I was quite banged up from having been a long time in the birth canal and having been forceps-delivered.

I do not know if he was disappointed that I was a girl. What I do know is that I felt bad when Mack was born and I, at 18 months old, sensed that I was being replaced as Number One.

Daddy's life was marked by huge losses. He describes what happened in his "Recollections for My Children":

The night Dad brought his wife and new son home from the hospital, he was burned to death. As I write this, I cannot believe that all of this could happen to a young man who was a leader in his community. How did he get to be an officer in a bank at what must have been in his early twenties? He was a good man, a happy man, and helped all his family and the community. It was always best not to think of it, and the president of the dry goods store where I worked on a summer job said, "Wylie, just go back to work and work hard. That's the only thing that will erase what has happened and get you back to normal. There's nothing you can do about what has happened." This is the first time I have ever written about what happened and the words come through a lot of sadness. How much can one family stand? It's good that we all had our religion [Presbyterian] to give us strength. I did go to work and didn't stop–until I retired.

I treasure these words. They show me his admiration for his father, his deep sadness at his untimely death and they let me see the strong advice he got from his boss. That advice was reinforced when his relatives told him to forget that the tragedy ever happened and to never think about it again. I believe that this is what he tried to do. He buried all that grief. It was frozen inside him and perhaps only came out in negative ways over the years.

My relationship with Daddy was difficult. I expected him to appreciate me and my accomplishments. He always seemed irritated or angry. At home, I bucked him at every opportunity.

Resolving my part in our relationship took a long time. In adulthood, my attitude toward him began to soften. In the 1970's, I went to Oklahoma City to work on Children's Beginning Experience. I invited Mama and Daddy to come from Taos, New Mexico, to visit family and to see me. During that visit Daddy asked me to go with him to select upholstery for his car. What happened as we drove all over Oklahoma City was miraculous. He drove me to all the houses, including the one that burned, in which he had lived. He courageously told me of his childhood and teenage years. I began to really understand him. Until then, I had just felt attacked or ignored. I had never seen his viewpoint. By God's grace, I was willing to hear his pain, thus giving me insight into his tragic youth.

But understanding him was not enough. I needed to forgive him. The first step in the forgiveness process came in 1982 on my way back from my sabbatical in New Zealand when Father Guy said "Forgiveness is the one grace that God will always give us if we pray for it." I began then to pray for it. I implored God for the grace to forgive Daddy.

The actual forgiveness came when I was at L'Arche in the 1990's. I went to the Trappist monastery for the retreat with our community. During the reconciliation service I approached the Abbot with one thing in mind: to ask for the grace to forgive Daddy. When I confessed that, the abbot looked at me and said—yes, those same words as Père Standard back in Belgium—"My precious child," then he continued, "Jesus has already forgiven your father and He is doing that in you right now. Let Him." I felt a great weight lifted from my heart. I am sure that Père Standard—now in heaven—had interceded for me and was chuckling. I'm also sure that Mama, who had had a hard time with Wylie, interceded for me and was smiling.

After forgiving Daddy, I wanted to make amends for not having forgiven him for so many years. That came to me in the opportunity I had to care for an old man—namely Bill Downey at L'Arche. I cared for

Bill with love and joy, and, in doing so, cared for Daddy. It was that simple.

After I left L'Arche in 1998 and moved to Wichita Falls, Daddy's memory began to fail. I called him twice a week. We had a good conversation each time. He was very proud that Wichita Falls had a Scripps-Howard newspaper (he never forgot that) and he said "I love you and I'm proud of you and thank you for calling. I really appreciate that, Jonie." These phone calls confirmed our healed relationship.

Before I went to New Zealand and Australia for the Regional Conference in September 2001, I went in June for a good visit with Daddy. He was still in Assisted Living at the Montebello. For some subconscious reason, I didn't feel emotionally up to going to see him alone, so I asked my cousin, Marcia, to meet me in Albuquerque.

I took the treasured family "Indian Photo Album" of Daddy's childhood. His eyes lit up when he saw it and he told me about the people in each picture. Marcia was very interested in the photos, many of which were of her mother, Dorothea Lou, as a baby and little girl. Dorothea Lou was Daddy's youngest sister, who had been left without mother or father at a young age. She looked sad in those photos. Looking at them with Marcia helped me understand even more clearly what the family life of my father must have been like. I realized that this blended family had a lot of difficult times. The photos showed two teenage boys (my father and his older brother) and little Dorothea Lou surrounded by a loving extended family. Then there was the last photograph of his mother, Marcia, with little Dorothea Lou, and the last picture of his father—a young man in the church choir. As Daddy paged through the album he talked about each event. His voice cracked as he told the stories. I taped what he said, so that I could identify all the old photographs.

We photocopied that old album, so that Marcia could take these memories home with her. She made a special little green album for Daddy, so he could live back there in his past. His face lit up and his eyes twinkled each time he looked at the photos of his mother and father and all the family, of Aunt Bessie, Uncle Mont and especially Coonie. I was grateful for that healing visit, a special gift from God!

Daddy had been having serious and bloody falls and had severe short-term memory failure. Part of me felt really sad about his drastic inabilities and another bigger part saw that he was peaceful and didn't seem depressed. He always knew me and I think he did a good job of maintaining any independence he could manage. He was much weaker and thinner than he had been when I visited in January, but he was in good spirits and had a twinkle in his eyes.

On December 7, 2001, my brother, Charlie, phoned from Daddy's room, now in Health Care at the Montebello, to say that Daddy had kidney failure and congestive heart failure and that he was sleeping all the time. He had weeks, not months, to live. The doctors told Charlie that he'd probably die in his sleep with no pain. I talked to Daddy and he was pleased to hear from me.

I thanked God for transforming this precious child of His into a gentle old man. God responded, "I transform everyone. In Wylie's case it is very evident; in others it is not so evident. I not only offer transformation to each one, I pursue them. My job is love and where I am, there is no time. So I'm very patient. Think often of my pursuit of each one. I pursue you, all the people you are with and your enemies."

I decided to go visit Daddy. God gave me a wonderful dream preparing me for Daddy's death. I was in a room full of clutter and chaos. Then it was transformed into a place of prayer with beautiful art and lovely contemplative people meditating. They were focused on a spiritual reality. They were all Buddhists and were living on another plane of existence. Someone was playing a harpsichord. Then my dream shifted. I was in a church where women were talking loudly and decorating with ugly artificial flowers. That was such a contrast to the real beauty created by the contemplatives. I woke up from this dream with the certitude that Mama, a contemplative, would be going with me on this trip to say goodbye to Daddy.

When I went on December 15, Daddy was asleep. So I just sat and prayed and looked around his room. It had a large window. The photo of Mama with the dog, Nikki, was close to him. Mama often chuckled as she said, "We [Nikki and I] look alike," and they did. Daddy's painting of Valdez Valley in the snow with the little houses and church, his last painting of the Navajo woman sitting with her horse, and one of his mission paintings were on the walls. The collage of Aunt Sally's kitchen and bathroom, and his favorite–the Indian drummer–were there. He was surrounded by all his favorite things. It was a comfortable room and looked like Daddy.

God spoke to me. "I'm taking good care of your daddy and easing your grief. I am with him, inside of him and taking him by the hand into the next life, life eternal where he will not only be with me but with his mother and father and Aunt Bessie and all who loved him and Aunt Sally and Uncle Paul. Now, you let go of the unfinished stuff of your life. I have given you incredible gifts through your struggle with your dad–gifts of compassion. You are giving these gifts to others."

I went for my last goodbye to Daddy on December 17, the first day of the "O Antiphons" preparing for Christmas. "The Desire of all nations is coming, and the house of the Lord will be filled with His glory."

I felt sad thinking that I would not see Daddy in his body again. His face was thinner, his hair chopped off short; his eyes still lit up. He was alert for the moment. We looked again at the old photos and he talked again about his mother. His feet and lower legs were swollen and his chest and throat were congested. I asked him if it hurt when he coughed and he said, "Yes, a little, but it's OK." He was totally transformed. I left while he was sleeping and blew him a kiss. I thanked God for my sister, Catharine, who thought of every detail in caring for him and in communicating with the staff at the Montebello. She was always there and the rest of us counted on her.

Catharine went to see him the evening of December 21. She left when he was sleeping peacefully. Just as she got to her home the nurse called to say he stopped breathing. He had what Mama always called a *Saint Joseph death* meaning: he died peacefully in his sleep.

Since Daddy died right before Christmas and I had just left him, I decided to go to Oklahoma City instead of to his funeral. I wanted to be with his relatives. On Christmas day, I drove to Mont and Lillian's. They were very connected to Daddy. They had come on their honeymoon to Fort Worth when I was a teenager. In their retirement they had built a vacation home near Mama and Daddy in Taos.

We looked at all the photos in the "Indian Photo Album" and we read Daddy's "Recollections for My Children." We laughed and cried as we read all those wonderful stories.

We wrote down all the addresses of his homes. We went on a pilgrimage, first to the ancestral burial ground next to First Presbyterian Church. I saw the gravestones of Daddy's parents, Marcia and Mack Stewart, his grandfather, John Graham Stewart, Aunt Grace and Uncle

Mont and their infant son, Aunt Bessie and Uncle Fred and Coonie and Flo. I remember well all of these people except his grandfather. Next we drove all over Oklahoma City to the places where Daddy had lived. That included the home where his father had been burned.

Then we returned to the kitchen table at Mont and Lillian's for our funeral celebration. It coincided with the time of the funeral in Albuquerque. We ended by singing "Amazing Grace" which I think captured Daddy's life.

I grieved by writing to and from Daddy, and through this written dialogue it became clear, from what Daddy wrote to me, that Heaven is where all is completed and transformed. Therefore it is useless to worry about having to finish everything on earth before we die.

Part of what I said to Daddy was, "I rejoice that you are with your dear mother and father and Aunt Bessie and Uncle Fred, and Coonie and Flo and all the rest of your family and Ewing and Dorothea Lou, too.....You and Mama gave life to such wonderful sons and daughters. We thank you for the life you gave us. I love you very much, after all our ups and downs. That last visit was the crowning grace which God gave us."

This is his letter back to me.

"Dearest Jonie, Let me tell you about Heaven. It was a big surprise and God was, is, so loving. Not in a 'soupy' kind of way. He shook my hand–a strong hand shake–and said–looking right into my eyes, 'Well done, Wylie. Welcome to Heaven.' Then I saw my parents. They looked the same as I remember and they knew everything about me and my life. It's a funny thing everyone looks about the same age, but they are all recognizable.

And there is no hurry here. I've already been fishing. The lakes and rivers are just incredible and we always catch big ones.

And Mama and I are just loving each other. (#35) All the hassles are gone. We are the best of ourselves.

Heaven is more beautiful than any place on earth that I've ever seen and all of it glows with a soft light. I see you and all on earth all the time, too, and I know now that God's power of love conquers all.

Love, Daddy"

Every time I watched Chariots of Fire I thought of Daddy. The runner and Daddy, both Scottish and Presbyterian, were contemporaries.

In the film the runner said, "God, you made me for a purpose and you also made me fast. When I run I give you pleasure. Not to run is to dishonor you. To run gives you honor." My father's gift was to be a superb newspaper man.

Daddy's unfinished grief and his consequent negative behavior, as I was growing up, had indirectly influenced the creation of the Beginning Experience, which is based on the principle that grief doesn't just go away. It must be gone through and dealt with. Daddy had been given the guidance of his era. He had been advised not to think of his mother and father and to work hard. Thus he had never expressed, gone through, or dealt with his grief directly. Instead, his grief had squeezed itself out in destructive ways. No one was at fault.

Something inside of me felt the imperative of giving people the opportunity that Daddy didn't have of working through their grief and coming to new life.

My experience of difficulty in forgiving Daddy may have sown the seeds of an another essential part of the Beginning Experience: namely that letting go and forgiving opens one to God's power of new life.

CHAPTER 19

BEGINNING EXPERIENCE DOWN UNDER

In addition to its healing, the Beginning Experience provided community for those who were thrust into aloneness. Its wonderful people welcomed me into their communities in faraway places.

In October, 2001 I went to New Zealand for the Regional Conference and then on to Australia. Everyone questioned my traveling so soon after 9-11, but I knew that there would be tightened security and that I would have the protection of the Holy Spirit.

After arriving in Auckland, I resurrected my body with a "cuppa" tea and toast with vegemite and then to the Olympics pool and hot tub, followed by a peppermint shower. That prepared me for an interview with the New Zealand Catholic newspaper and the long Asia Pacific Board Meeting. Long ago I had learned to get my body going and then never, never to go to bed before 10:00. That was always a sure cure for jet lag.

The Auckland conference began with Maori music and the most sacred Maori *Hongi*, the custom of nose touching–the exchange of breath. From that start I was filled with energy. I spoke in the keynote address about Daddy's frozen grief. All the workshops were designed to energize and celebrate the diversity of the groups from New Zealand, Australia and Singapore.

The climax was the presentation from the young people who spoke of how divorce or death affected, even traumatized, them. They spoke directly and honestly to their tearful parents. Afterward we gave them a standing ovation.

After the conference, I went to visit Anne and John Brier on whose farm I had lived in 1982. What an adventure to drop back on them every ten years. I reflected on how young we all were when I first knew them. (#34)

I went almost immediately to see John's parents, Mary and Doug. Their sons and daughters were rotating staying with them. What a community effort to care for their precious parents! They explained it simply: "It's payback time now." Mary was sick and Doug was waiting on her despite his frailty. That day he had been to a golf tournament of World War II vets, but had to leave because of weakness. He had waited a long time for the golf event and seemed to be energized by it, but it was too much for him. He looked extremely thin, translucent, and other worldly. Mary was resting but talked a lot about all her children. I prayed with them for my heavenly friend, Archangel Raphael, to intercede for them. That last visit with them was providential. Doug died soon after.

I was able to spend a few days with Anne and John. They were part of a group of couples who were discerning about farming for the joy of it as opposed to farming for material gain. The group shared ideas and dreams for creating a kind of sustainable community.

Besides feeding the tiny lambs by bottle in her "orphan" pen, Anne also moved the cattle from one paddock to another. On that particular day, Anne took the lead in her dune buggy and John and I followed in another. Some cattle were in the wrong place, so I watched Anne and the dogs work and John use his whistle to command them. That was quite an evolution from the "ancient" process of mustering that I had seen 20 years earlier on their Coromandel farm, when then, 2 year old Daniel, was learning how to command the dogs.

After my wonderful visit, Anne drove me back through the lava landscape to board a train to Wellington, where I would see significant friends and their grown children, especially Shirley, who had been on the original New Zealand team, having come to Hawaii in 1979.

Shirley took me to her daughter Pere's home for tea. Pere is a solo mom living with her daughter who is very bright and artistic. Pere seemed wise. She spoke of the upheaval and chaos in the world that is preceding a great transformation. I still remember the light in Pere's face and eyes. Her hope was contagious.

Shirley and I drove from Wellington on the North Island to Christchurch. She was shifting (moving) back after years working in the Beehive, New Zealand's famous capitol building. Her tiny car was stuffed with plants and treasures. After a spectacular ferry crossing we drove along the east coast of the South Island with the purple-blue Pacific on our left and the snow-capped Kaikoura Mountains on our right. We saw hundreds of sun-bathing seals and shared our lunch with fat sea gulls.

After arriving at Shirley's ancestral home in Christchurch, where Jo Lamia and I had spent that first night in November 1979, we were greeted by her unmarried son, Shane, her daughter, Fleur, with her 12 year old son. I had managed to catch up with most of Shirley's grown children: Pania, her daughter in Northern Ireland, and Pere with her daughter in Wellington. Now I had the chance to be with Shane and Fleur.

Shirley's garden was a paradise of native plants. Nearby at rugged Brighton Beach was the new pier and library, built in the form of a ship. It was glass on the ocean side. Inside were big chairs with headsets. Anyone could come sit, read, listen to music, or be calmed by the ocean. That was the beach where I had escaped the noise of the "boot boys" back in 1982.

I was quite anxious to see Noel and Veronica with whom I had spent a good part of my sabbatical. They always fixed a big breakfast on Sunday morning and invited everyone to come. It was the perfect time for me to visit. Almost everyone I had known from the past came and we had plenty of time to talk and catch up on ten years of living.

That evening I went with Alisoun to the Sunday evening service at her Lutheran church. It was a Celtic Circle for All Saints' and All Souls' Day in memory of those who had died in the past year. The reading was of Jacob tearing his garment over Joseph, his lost son. We too tore fabric, lamenting and grieving for someone we'd lost. We lit candles and put camellias in a bowl for each deceased person. The service ended with a sung blessing of Saint Patrick.

When I was introduced to speak, I simply asked them to live peace. That trip took place very soon after 9-11, and there was much fear of war.

Alisoun's home is surrounded by flowers. Her garden, which can be seen through the large windows in the living area, is a splendid array of Tree Ferns, Camellias, Azaleas, Rhododendron, Blue Bells, Lilies of the Valley, Irises, Lavender and Roses. All were in bloom.

She had invited a group of former Beginning Experience people to meet and to commit themselves to supporting the revival of the Christchurch team. I was very heartened by that meeting, seeing the love they showed for the ministry. I thought of the generations of teams who started Beginning Experience in faraway countries, trained their successors and then helped keep this ministry alive. As I listened to these wonderful people, I reflected on the mystery of Christ's dying and rising, not only in individual lives, but also for organizations and for our Beginning Experience teams. In some ways dying and rising reflects a normal cycle. But I always feel sad when teams die out. Since Jo and I had been in Christchurch as part of their pilot weekend, I was particularly saddened by its dying.

Next day, Jim Curnow came to collect me to go to his lavender farm at Waikuku. His partner, Joan, was on the riding mower. They gave me a grand tour of the farm: the trout stream running through it, the workroom where the helpers were making cuttings, the greenhouse and the lavender fields. I learned that working physically with lavender is very calming and healing.

Joan took me to the beach, where I sat for hours meditating on the ocean of God's love. I sat enthralled by the sights and sounds–the roar and then the gentle hiss, of the blue-green Pacific Ocean. The water was cold so I sat in a lawn chair in my swim suit and felt the cold water on my feet and the warm sun on my body–a glorious taste of Paradise.

Next morning, I sat on the step to wait, in the pre-dawn glow, for the sunrise–always a resurrection time for me.

That day, I visited with the Glenda's family. John, who had been a "boot boy" 20 years before, cried and cried when he saw me. He had lived in Perth, Australia, for many years and had such strong memories of me when he was age 18 and again at 28. Now at 38 he was married and happy. Glenda, his mother, owned a lavender farm in the city. Her daughters, Heather and Rosalie, lived close by with their children. John was the main worker on the farm. Rosalie was doing wonderful things teaching 7-year-olds about living in community–preparing them to live in our world. Heather was such a good mum: giving choices, speaking softly, setting boundaries and saying *no* gently.

What a profound experience! Young people I had known in 1982 had become caring, loving, transformed adults–gifts to New Zealand and to our world. Many of them were from 'solo' families.

At the end of my New Zealand stay, we all gathered at Noel and Veronica's to be together before I left and to recapture my time there.

(#21) We ate delicious barbeque in the garden. We were especially blessed with the full Autumnal Equinox moon.

The next day Noel took me to the airport for my flight to Australia. I reflected with him that New Zealand feels like home. As usual I cried as I said good-bye. On the flight God wrote to me: "Dearest Josephine, I *am* your HOME. Wherever you go I am surrounding you with love. Connect with me before, behind, above, below and inside. You can see a dim reflection of my love in the family you have in New Zealand, but always know that I am your constant companion–your beloved. All those you love and those who love you are a shadow of my love. There is no distance in my love, no time or space. To pray always simply means that you connect with me as the grounding of your life. Love, God."

AUSTRALIA

Coming into Hobart on the island of Tasmania reminded me of Ireland with its hills and patchwork of green. That evening we went to a large gathering at the Catholic Center of all who were on Beginning Experience teams from its Tasmanian inception in 1988. I was able to visit with little groups.

Next day after answering questions at the local board meeting, Mike, president of the Regional Board, took me to his home. He was a scholar of Ancient Egyptian Civilization and had decorated his home with rugs and artifacts from Egypt. The rugs hanging on his walls were not tapestries. They were all created by hand in non-geometric representational designs of life in Egypt.

In this setting he took out his files of the Australian teams and tried to update me on each situation. He explicitly talked about each team living the *Vision and Mission*. He was preparing me for the tragic situation in Darwin. Next day after visiting the Catholic Center offices, I flew to Melbourne.

Jan met me in Melbourne and we toured the marvelous port city: its beaches, bridges, industrial area, container port, harbor, water front homes. We ended up at Massala's Italian Restaurant where the Beginning Experience team of five gathered. I was able to visit with each of them, because they rotated chairs. We talked about re-vitalizing their small team. We ended at 11:00 p.m. and it was well worth the late hour.

Next morning, after a good sleep, Jan and I went to the Aquatic Center, where I enjoyed the bubbly hot tub and water running for 30 minutes. I was refreshed.

That afternoon we celebrated the Melbourne Cup. That was *the* sport event of Australia. I hadn't planned it this way–to be in Melbourne the very day of the race. I recalled when Jo Lamia and I arrived in Sydney the first time in November 1979 and our driver suddenly stopped and parked the car, because it was the custom for all of Australia to stop–full stop–for the running of the Melbourne Cup.

Then, November 2001, I was actually in Melbourne for the Cup. While in New Zealand, I had seen an interview with Sheila Laxon, the trainer of Ethereal, and had decided that I would have placed $2.00 on Ethereal. During most of the race she was nowhere to be seen, nor was she on the listings of the top five in the race. It was only in the last half mile of the 2-mile course that she appeared and started coming up from the back like lightning to second place and then ahead at the finish. I was pleased, really pleased for her, for New Zealand and for the woman trainer in her big-brimmed black hat with her broken cell phone, held together with rubber bands because Ethereal had stepped on it. Trainer, horse and jockey were all New Zealand women.

That same day Jan and I left for Phillip Island to see the Parade of the Fairy Penguins. We ventured down to the ramp to wait for the penguins. The hills surrounding the beaches were filled with burrows containing the baby penguins. The parent penguins went out each day to feed and returned each night filled with fish to feed their young. There were elaborate pavilions and ramps from which tourists watched the parent penguins come ashore and start "calling out" to find the exact burrow and their chicks.

The young did not know the call of their parents, but the parents knew the cry of their chicks and went back to their exact burrow each night bringing enough food in their bellies, which they regurgitated to feed their chicks. Sea gulls flew around for possible stray tidbits as the penguins waddled up the beach. Mostly the penguins were just so cute. The parents were really small with bluish white breasts, dark coats and little flippers.

Driving back Jan and I discussed the difficult situation in Darwin. Once at home, Jan further helped prepare me by lighting candles, meditating with me, and listening to a CD repeating Alleluias and Kyries. She talked to me about complete trust that dispels fear. And God wrote telling me He was sending His Spirit into me to give me courage and to take away fear. He also suggested that I think of the Fairy Penguins when I felt helpless. In all the surrounding clamor they clearly heard and faithfully fed their young. I flew to Darwin with peace.

At the Darwin airport, I thought I'd lost my friends, Gemma and Ben. My luggage was the last off and then they appeared. We drove to their home through coconut palms and tropical vegetation. Next day, Gemma and I went to a beautiful bay looking out on the ocean in the direction of Indonesia.

We sat in lawn chairs in a pile of what looked like gravel. It turned out to be tiny hermit crabs. There were also many beautiful stones: yellow ochre, burnt orange, red and white stones. Gemma explained that the Aboriginal people crush these rocks to make body paint. There were many broken pieces of coral.

Gemma drove around the bay to show me the World War II bunkers built to protect Darwin from Japanese attack. Actually the Japanese bombed Darwin from the south. Many were killed there in 1942. That was one of a number of towns in northern Australia that had been bombed by the Japanese.

We drove through Aboriginal communities, sacred land. Many live in tall grass like nomads, but many live in communities with housing set up by the Australian government. Gemma is sensitive to them, seeing their health problems, their alcohol problems and their deep spirituality.

Before our meeting with the Darwin team, we went for a wonderful cool swim in a tropical garden surrounded by tiny finches and peace doves. I spent a few minutes praying and collecting myself in preparation for the meeting. The priest and sister who ran Beginning Experience in Darwin had asked for the meeting. As the founder of this ministry, I wanted to stress unity and continuity from its founding to the present time. I wanted to explore how to heal and preserve the integrity of this precious gift from God.

In the meeting room, Gemma and I set out candles and played soothing music. From the outset the priest tried to take over. Neither he nor the Sister who directed their "beginning experience" had ever made the copyrighted Beginning Experience weekend. Therefore, they were not peers in terms of this ministry. They saw no need to be connected with the International Ministry Center or to be accountable to the International Board or to the Asia Pacific Regional Board. They fully intended to continue presenting their version of beginning experience. They told us of their intention to do so and of their belief in self-directed autonomy for their local team.

The whole affair left me feeling sad and deeply concerned for the safety and welfare of those who had been or would be participants in their version of the beginning experience. I felt angry and worried because a priest and nun ignored the danger to people who were extremely vulnerable during a time of grief. They seemed to put their limited knowledge above that of those who had designed and guided a researched program with built-in safe-guards.

Gemma and Ben were still ready to do everything possible to start over – but that was not possible. I was extremely saddened by the closing of the Darwin team and the subsequent void left in Darwin. The Asia/Pacific Regional Board was left with cleaning up the mess.

Next day I slept until I got up without an alarm. Despite the tension of the previous day's meeting, I felt rested and full of energy. The day with Gemma and Ben was filled with an immersion into Aboriginal art starting at Nungalinya, the Aboriginal Art School. We saw the students' exquisite hand printed fabrics on display for the up-coming Christmas sale.

We then went to the large museum for the permanent Aboriginal Art exhibit. All paintings tell a story–some are dream time stories. One story was about the way that death came into the world. The wife of the great leader took her baby to the sea and there she met her lover, and forgot her child who died there. Her husband's wrath was great and thus death came to humanity. The story was told in detail in the paintings.

All too soon, it was time to move on from Darwin. My final words to Gemma and Ben were about their pain over the Darwin team, and I hoped they would put all their energy into love, "the love without which the world would cease to exist." I have kept close to them through e-mail and in 2006 we were together in Winnipeg, Canada at the International Convention.

As I flew to Cairns God spoke again, "Let go of Darwin's tragedy and now just have fun. Enjoy my wonderful world. Let go of the past and live only in the present moment. I love you and I've managed all. All is well. All is very well. All will be well." I knew that God was holding me.

Since I realized late the night before my departure to Cairns, that I had made a typographical error on my itinerary of p.m. instead of a.m., I phoned to say I was arriving in the morning instead of at night. The airport at Cairns was exceptional. The wheel chair attendant whisked me through a long passage with floor-to-ceiling paintings of underwater sea life and underwater sounds. I went from there into the arms of the Cairns Beginning Experience team.

My home in Cairns was beautiful with swimming pool and a waterfall outside my bedroom. I started off with a swim in the pool and then sat by the waterfall. I just rested listening to the soothing sounds of falling water and seeing the water lilies and gold fish in the little pool. It seemed to me to be a physical way of letting go of the past.

After lunch, some of the Cairns team took me to a session of "Continued Beginnings" (the follow through program after the weekend) at Our Lady of Good Counsel Church in Innesfail. We drove through valleys, between mountains covered with sugar cane, papaya and bananas.

The session started with a song about coming home to God. I felt at home with these people. All team and participants renewed their transforming time at the Beginning Experience. The simple sharing was on how they had been freed to love themselves and others and God. It was well worth the trip and was an additional gift to me, since I had said I was arriving in the evening.

After we got back home, my hostess brought me a tray with a gardenia and a cup of tea and then gave me a massage, during which I went to sleep. Next day, Sunday, the readings at Mass were of the Resurrection. I felt immersed in the resurrection and Our Lady of Good Counsel and taken care of by God through these dear people, by all their touches of love.

A couple, who met through Beginning Experience, asked me to bless their new home. It was a lovely yellow frame house with hardwood floors. I blessed every room and all the walls. I spoke to them of Julian of Norwich, the hermitess who told those who came to her that "All is well, all is very well, all will be well!"

That afternoon, we went to the 15th Anniversary Celebration of the Cairns Beginning Experience. All past participants had been invited. Many came from the surrounding towns. Father John Butcher had been their "pastor" all this time.

I simply loved talking to them. There was such eye contact and energetic response. At the potluck meal, out on the veranda, I visited with each group, going from table to table asking them to network with each other. The celebration ended with a birthday cake with 15 candles. That evening, with just the Cairns team, we gathered for another potluck, Father John Butcher recited from memory the epic poem by Banjo Patterson, *Man from Snowy River*.

I came to understand on this trip why Australia is so loyal to the United States. This loyalty goes back to World War II when the United States military saved Australia from the Japanese. My hostess drove me up to the highest point above Cairns to a monument giving the distance and directions to Guadalcanal, Midway, and the Coral Sea. I recalled all these terrible battles, which I had heard about on our Philco radio and had seen in the theaters at the weekly Pathe News. For those Australians living on their Northeast coast in 1942, those islands and that war were very close.

And, of course, we went to the Great Barrier Reef and down in the yellow submarine into the coral reefs. We only saw a tiny segment of this extensive wonder of the world. The submarine provided an air-conditioned immersion into the Great Barrier Reef. What an experience of the immensity of God! Thus ended my stay in Cairns. What beauty and what compassionate loving people!

In Brisbane, Esma, my long time friend and the heart of the Beginning Experience in Australia, met me at the airport. She had been living by choice for several years with people, instead of having her own place. She was literally homeless, having let go of a place to call "home." At that time, she was living with a young couple who had each made the Young Adult Beginning Experience, had been on that team and had later married. They had asked Esma to house sit for them when they went for a magical Christmas to Germany. That was how she came to live with them.

Esma entertained me by bringing out all her posters and photos of Beginning Experience in Brisbane and Singapore, where she had helped start that team. She had remembrances from all the

International Conventions and Regional Conferences over the past years. In addition, she was hostess to many people from North America and England and Ireland who accepted her invitation and hospitality. She was a veritable "heartbeat" for connecting the world of the Beginning Experience in the Asia/Pacific with the United States and with Great Britain/Ireland. What an experience of connection in time and space to years of teams and people! I experienced through her the mustard seed grown to fullness.

Esma and I went to the theatre district, where she works part time in the administration office. We met her friend for lunch there and then went on the boardwalk along the Brisbane River. The city itself was across the river. On our side, was the art district. All the theatres and museums were located there, and, connecting all, were lightweight aluminum lattice arbors covered with bright blooming Bougainvillea. That area was enchanting–full of people enjoying their beautiful city.

As a gift, Esma gave me a lovely "throw" that she had made out of wool and silk. She "felted" them in a process of crisscrossing wool fibers, adding raw silk and then pressing them on a lightweight cotton backing with boiling water and soap. As the wool dried, it shrank and rippled up the cotton. It was lightweight and warm. She created a floral design of Australian Wattle in yellow and green on a white background.

That evening we dashed off to the Mercy Center for a gathering of Brisbane Beginning Experience people from 1983 to 2001. Representatives from each year were there. Many of them I had met at International Conventions in Denver, New Orleans, Detroit, Houston, Fort Worth and Omaha and at the Regional Conference in Auckland. What an experience of God continuing to connect us all in this family of divorced and widowed people!

It was a superb gathering! I sat down to give my talk and all eyes were alert and loving. I stressed, again, our worldwide reach and the importance of staying connected with those in Australia. Many came afterward to speak to me in gratitude. Esma had brought her photos and posters. Esma was obviously pleased with the event and all the connecting and celebrating. What a farewell to Brisbane!

My last place to visit was Sydney. Sister Mary Constable, then 82, and Sister Marie, age 74, met me at the airport. They lived in a state house (Government housing) at the bottom of a hill. It was very clean and nicely decorated, three bedrooms, and a bath and a half, and an exquisite garden. They ministered to their neighbors in whatever way they saw, giving them rides up the steep hill to the bus line, conducting a Bible-sharing group, being caring neighbors by welcoming all who came to their door. I was impressed with these two dear women who were in tune with the reality of the lives of those near them. Next day, one of the "originals" from 1979 came over for a visit. Jo Lamia had loved her when we stayed with her in 1979. She spoke about her full life, her involvement with her beloved Hunters Hill neighborhood, her teaching aerobics and stress management, her two knee replacements and now her diminishing health. Her face was beautiful and translucent. We re-membered.

The best part of that Sydney visit was riding the ferry with Sister Mary Constable as we had done in 1979, to the Central Queue of Sydney. The blue Jacarandas were in full bloom. The Opera House was formidable. We just goofed off for several hours, shopping and eating fish 'n chips and visiting.

That evening, a large group of Beginning Experience people gathered at Sacred Heart Church. It was a great event and they all felt supported and renewed in their ministry. I thanked God for giving me energy and using me as an instrument of His compassion. Sister Mary Constable was a warrior. She was there in Hawaii in August 1979. Despite her failing eyesight, she has continued to minister to the divorced, widowed and marginalized ever since.

I knew that I would probably not see her again on earth. The day I left she wore a light blue dress and was heading off to represent her Mother General at a meeting. She called a cab for me after she carried my bags down the stairs, and I went to the airport and was on my way to Hawaii.

Ginny, from the original Hawaii team, met me. November 16, 2001, was my "gift day" in Hawaii. We went to Paradise Cove, near Honolulu. Since all beaches in Hawaii were by law open to the public, my gift was to sit under a palm tree and to spend hours in the crystal clear water amid the fish. The ocean became once again a metaphor of God's love.

After that Ginny drove me to see the surfers. We watched the huge translucent, aquamarine waves with dozens of surfers riding them

146

down. It was like in the travelogues, but that was for real. I thought of a young man from New Zealand who was a surfer. He traveled the world, making just enough money with odd jobs to support his surfing. How many young and not so young people lived that life!

Then we showered and got ready for the Beginning Experience weekend. It was held at Saint Anthony's Retreat Center, run by the Sacred Heart Sisters, who built it in 1904 as an orphanage for the children whose parents had died of leprosy (Hansen's disease). They had turned it into a retreat center. In the Guest House I slept very well. The roosters crowed even during the night. I thanked God for this lovely space and time to reflect on my month in New Zealand and Australia and time to rest. I followed the flow of the weekend, listening to all the presentations, but instead of being part of a small group, I did my own processing. What a marvelous transition time from what I'd been doing, into what was ahead.

During my private time of reflecting, I saw how this particular trip was completing the circle of my Beginning Experience life. It became abundantly clear to me that, in my life and in the lives of each person who was part of these trips, God had been living His life in us. Jo Lamia was very present to me during the reflection time. I could actually hear her voice speaking to me.

That trip was a gathering of people that Jo and I had met and loved 22 years ago. I saw the unmistakable influence of the Beginning Experience on them. I knew that Jo was with me on this trip, rejoicing in the harvest of the seeds we had planted years earlier. That trip sharpened my appreciation of all communities. Being with all those Beginning Experience people gave me a clear view that each person was an infinitely important part of the whole.

I rejoiced to see how many young people, offspring of divorce and death, had become peacemakers. With stars in their eyes and love in their hearts they worked for peace in our violent world. I was reminded of the young people in New Zealand who worked for peace, gathering weekly at the Bridge of Peace in Christchurch.

After the weekend, some of the old timers from 1979 came to reconnect with me. Eddie, who had taken photos of every single weekend since 1979, came. He was Puerto Rican. His parents came to Hawaii by way of San Francisco. He was a boy working in the sugar cane fields on December 7, 1941, when the Japanese bombed Pearl Harbor. He saw the planes with the orange sun on the side and saw the black smoke bellowing up, a memory that has lived in him. After Eddie died I considered him a special intercessor for Beginning Experience.

The Hawaiians exuded a spirit of hospitality. They called it Aloha. Everyone was embraced, accepted and "leied" with garlands of sweet smelling flowers.

On the plane coming home, God wrote to me: "It's all about abundance of life and love and synchronicity. I've blessed you with great gifts. Have no fears of the future."

Somehow this month long adventure was for me a huge transition from a small view to an immense view. I saw the expansion of my vision through the lens of time and space. I had seen the start and growth of this ministry in Australia and in New Zealand over a period of 20 years. The trip had been a journey with God, exploring the landscape of His magnificent world. More than that, it was a journey with the loving people of the Beginning Experience. It was also my being loved by them whose lives were forged in suffering and resurrection.

CHAPTER 20

BEGINNING EXPERIENCE OF GREAT BRITAIN AND IRELAND

As I packed, I thought of Jesus instructions to the disciples to go forth with just one tunic and a pair of sandals and I realized how complex my life had gotten. I saw that when I ventured out of my comfort zone, I "had to" take a lot of stuff for my daily existence and I was aware of aging.

In going to England, Ireland and Northern Ireland at this time, I wanted to be with the Beginning Experience people at their 2003 regional conference in Leeds, England. Bridie Gallagher had invited me, really pleaded with me, to attend the Young People's Beginning Experience in Derry, Northern Ireland, which she had scheduled after the conference. Personally I hoped to discover the secret of the Celts which I found so evident in the Irish Beginning Experience team people. I wanted to make a pilgrimage throughout Ireland to experience Celtic spirituality. I had not planned any of the details of visiting monastic villages or holy shrines. I left that up to God and His abundant gift of synchronicity.

I had read and absorbed a little of Celtic spirituality. I knew that it was about love of nature, respect for art and poetry, living hospitality and being in touch with the spirit world. I knew that Saint Patrick converted Ireland by laying Christianity over, not destroying, the Celtic spirituality that he found there. He wrote a journal, *Confessions*, about his divine call to convert Ireland and what it cost him to respond to that challenge. I related to him because, I, too wrote a lot in my journal. With those intentions in mind I flew to London.

I had a long wait in London's Heathrow Airport before I connected with Kathleen, the executive director of the Beginning Experience. That city and its airports and shuttles were the crossroads of the world. Watching and listening, I saw the world pass by within a couple of hours: people from the Philippines, Romania, Greece, Japan,

Denmark, Germany, Israel, Palestine, Lebanon, Iran, Syria, and Egypt. I heard English spoken with many accents.

Everyone walked fast and determinedly, but the cleaners in the restroom area were having fun like the grandmother from Poland who was living in London, to be close to her grown children. She appeared happy–joking with a fellow worker from Poland.

I met a String Ensemble from Vienna on their way from touring England en route to Mexico and Los Angeles. The group consisted of Korean, Russian and Austrian men. I loved my day of "people-watching."

I connected with Kathleen. We flew to Leeds and crammed our luggage, circus-style, into a tiny vehicle. Sister Catherine–long time leader in England for Beginning Experience–was our hostess for a marvelous dinner and a good night's sleep. Next morning, I worked out at a charming Tudor Spa. Glass walls provided a great view of lovely trees full of magpie birds. On the ride through Leeds I was able to appreciate the quaintness of that University City.

When we walked through the doors of Hensley Hall into the Regional Conference, there were two striking banners of bright flames on dark backgrounds and the text of the "Vision of Beginning Experience:" a hurting people healed, transformed and free again to love. It was a stunning sight. We saw a display of postcards sent by each team from around the world, including the waterfall postcard I had sent from Wichita Falls, Texas.

The opening ceremony was a splendid acknowledgement of each team. Then the Master of Ceremonies introduced me stating, the colonists are here to speak to us. I responded emphasizing how our Vision of Beginning Experience gives us freedom not from the British but by passing through grief to new life and the ability to love again.

The focus of the conference was on the integrity of the Beginning Experience process and on the introduction of new training materials. Kathleen gave a marvelous explanation of the power and value of words and of writing. I spoke of a new ideal within "The Vision"–an ideal of *compassionate listening* which goes beyond *empathic listening*. I explained that compassionate listening is the "heart to heart" listening of someone who has love and understanding of another person because they share a similar grief. It is the essence of the peer, like-to-like ministry.

Each team wrote out their problem situations which were then categorized. After lunch, we had a very lively session responding to different and yet common situations. It was one of the finest examples of group interaction that I've ever observed. Everyone felt a common bond–a focus in the same direction.

The Saturday night party at that convention was fun. I loved being with them dancing and laughing. Who would ever believe that each one had such a sad story of depression, isolation, rejection, abuse or despair? I loved seeing the happy faces of the old, the young, and the middle aged and seeing the short, tall, fat, thin doing the Irish and Scottish dances! Toward the end of that party, I just happened to meet Sandra, who told me she lived five minutes from the airport in London, and invited me to stay with her on my way back home. That was another little miracle of synchronicity!

The Eucharistic celebration to end the Conference was in the large, airy chapel of the Little Sisters of the Poor. The Bishop was the celebrant. He gave a wonderful homily on the Gifts of the Spirit. After Communion he warmly thanked us for this important healing ministry. He presented the Certificate of Certification to the Dundalk team, which had waited patiently through many trials to be certified. I said I was thrilled to be with my "grandchildren."

After lots of photos, hugs and goodbyes, we left for the drive south on the motorways to Plymouth. Christine, my hostess, drove and Ann sat in the back seat as navigator. We talked and talked, telling Beginning Experience stories. We were so full of the wonder of how we got to the weekend, and the transformation inside of us during the weekend and the spontaneous "connecting" which happened all through the conference.

At one point, I wanted to chuck my apple core and banana peel out the window for the birds. Christine said, "Let's put it in a plastic. I don t think there will be any birds landing on the motorway."

It was dark when we got off the last motorway and on to the tiny roads that led to Christine's home in Cristow. We drove through tunnels of hedgerows. I later learned that these hedgerows were hundreds of years old.

The next day we were off through the tunnels of hedgerows to Exeter to the public pool. Men and women were in the same shower and dressing room. After my vigorous workout in the water and massaging my feet in the strong jets, I contemplated my plan to shower. It was quite a feat to shower and then get to the dressing room without "streaking." Everyone else seemed blasé about this arrangement. I guess my Puritan blood made me a bit squeamish.

That evening the team gathered for an Agape. It consisted of sharing two scripture passages and bread and wine. Each person poured wine from a pitcher into his/her goblet, saying what gifts Beginning Experience had given them. Then each one poured the wine back into the pitcher saying what gifts they had given to the ministry. So the gifts were symbolically mingled. Then we shared the bread and wine.

After the Agape, I spoke of the responsibility we each had of cherishing the treasure of Beginning Experience by being faithful to its process. I reflected on the power of God when He inspired Jo Lamia and me to write the process down.

The next day, we went to Plymouth to the Mayflower Steps. It was the exact place from which the Puritan Pilgrims set sail for Massachusetts in 1620. That embarkation point for many colonizing groups was situated under a massive citadel. It was marked by British and American flags. I sketched it, so it is emblazoned in my memory.

Leaving Plymouth we drove along a seaside resort and onto the motorway to Buckfast Abbey which had been built in 1081 but later Henry VIII had forced the monks to leave. They had returned in the 1800's and restored it. Locals refer to it as fast Buck because of the enormous amount of money collected to restore it. The grounds were beautiful and the great Church was magnificent with lots of little side altars and shrines.

Before I left that part of England I wanted to sketch an old church and cemetery. The last day in Cristow, I sketched Saint James Church and Cemetery. I sat under a tree and pulled this church and cemetery into my being and out onto my sketch pad. The experience of drawing was personal for me—more profound than taking a photograph. I reserved taking pictures for people's faces.

On October 10, I left England on Air Wales. We were an hour late leaving Plymouth bound for Dublin. Because of strong headwinds we landed in Cardiff, Wales, for re-fueling. I overheard, out the open plane door, a workman say, "Bloody hell, can't they ever learn to put enough petrol for this trip?" I was thankful that we were saved from going empty into the ocean.

Father Sebastian, the head of Buckfast Abbey, was on that same plane. I saved a place for him next to me. Christine had told me that he was a great organist and composer of monastic music. He was on his way to Galway, his home town, to play a concert, but because we were so late he missed his connection. I took that situation into my "control" and arranged a new flight for him.

While Father Sebastian and I chatted on the flight over, I reviewed my itinerary for visiting Celtic places and monastic villages in Ireland. He suggested and wrote down as a must-see: CLONMACNOISE.

The first place on my pilgrimage was Glendalaugh (pronounced Glendalock). Willie and Helen drove me. I took their names as a wee gift from God since my parents are Wylie and Helen. We drove along the Irish coast and through green patchwork fields. We arrived and viewed a film on monasticism in Ireland which explained that Ireland was the mother earth for villages of real people living around monasteries.

We walked through the ruins of the monastic community. I was awed by the remains of the finest round tower in Ireland with its perfectly straight walls. It had once been used as a bell-and-watchtower. The ruins of the large Cathedral were in the center with its splendid stone tabernacle. Saint Kevin's Chapel was small and completely intact with its walls made of small stones and its roof of larger stones. Our guide pointed out some ancient carved graffiti on a window frame.

I sat on the cemetery wall and sketched Saint Kevin's Church, while Willie and Helen walked up to the famous twin lakes. As I sketched I thought of all the men, women and children and the monks who had lived community life here in the seventh century, the early days of Catholic Ireland, soon after St. Patrick.

Next day was my 72nd birthday. My hostess had a lovely breakfast for me with her poems and a card. After Mass, at the Poor Claires' Convent, Maureen and Sister Rhoda, who had promised in Leeds to take me on a pilgrimage for my birthday, arrived.

We started by going to Saint Michen's in Dublin where the first public performance of Handel's *Messiah* had taken place. Father Sebastian had told me that he had played on that same organ on which Handel had played.

Sister Rhoda, Maureen and I journeyed by the back road to Newgrange. I had never heard of Newgrange. It was a huge burial mound surrounded by smaller burial mounds pre-dating the pyramids of Egypt and Stonehenge in England. It was 5000 years old. Ancient people rolled huge stones on logs for hundreds of miles to form that large cave-like structure. The narrow entrance was so exactly designed that once a year, at the Winter solstice, a shaft of sunlight pierced through the passage lighting up the innermost wall. The ancient ones knew the sun and moon times and arranged their religious festivals to celebrate those times. Saint Patrick used Celtic celebrations to teach the Christian feasts. For example, he taught that the Sun of Justice came at the time of the winter solstice to give light to the darkest time of the year.

The entrance to the Newgrange Cave was decorated with small granite cobbles. A closer look showed a wide border of the entrance covered with white quartz cobbles. At the base was an enormous carved stone representing the Boyne River valley. I thought about the thousands of years when the Celtic people celebrated the sun here. I could see Saint Patrick speaking of the sun, and I could hear my grandmother saying, "If I had been a pagan I would have worshipped the sun." And I thought of my appreciation of the rising sun and my fascination with the rising full moon especially over the ocean.

Sister Rhoda, Maureen and I went to Slane to the hill where Saint Patrick had lit the great Easter bonfire. Since the king of Tara had forbidden any outdoor fires, he dispatched his chariots and charioteers to capture the person responsible for that fire. Tara was the great hill across the valley from Slane. The king's men intended to kill Saint Patrick. Instead, Saint Patrick took the non-violent approach and spoke to them about lighting the Easter fire and celebrating Christ's resurrection. Those men were converted and went back to the king, who then allowed Saint Patrick to continue his work.

We continued our pilgrimage to Saint Brigid's shrine and washed our faces and hands in her stream and drank the water. Then at Mount Olivet Center, where Sister Rhoda was the director, we gathered with the Dundalk team for a lovely salad supper. I spoke to them about the power of Beginning Experience which is in letting go of past hurts with Christ and moving to transformation and resurrection. That team had gracefully demonstrated the process in their patient waiting for certification. They gave me a lovely framed Saint Brigid's "shrine," containing one of her oat-stem Celtic crosses. They drove me back to Dublin.

Kathleen Murphy arrived in Dublin. I was happy to see her and to go on part of my Irish pilgrimage with her. First stop was Naas to find Saint David's Church. Nothing but the bell tower remained. It was Norman construction. Saint David was a contemporary of Saint Brigid and Saint Kevin. We walked around the ancient cemetery.

When we tried to return by the same gate through which we had entered, it was locked tight. Panic set in. We were afraid of being captive in a cemetery for hours. I called out to two women who were passing by. There was a number to call for the code to unlock the gate. One woman whipped out her cell phone, called the number and obtained the code. We got out. We laughed about being locked in Saint David's cemetery.

Even though I had already been to Saint Brigid's shrine in the north, I wanted to visit her well near Kildare, but when we got there Saint Brigid's Church was locked. No one seemed to know anything about that famous well. Eventually, we found it. There were hundreds of prayer requests and scraps of fabric and other tokens of healing in a tree. Her statue, beside a little stream, was lovely, depicting her holding a flame. She wore no veil.

Dublin's team gathered that night. Forty members sat in a circle. I spoke to them about Jo Lamia as the heartbeat of this ministry and again focused on the value of writing. Each time I experienced the continued workings of God's Spirit through me and my words, I was humbled and awed. The time in Ireland was a deep, spiritual time for me, connecting me with the Celtic traditions and re-enforcing the initial focus and integrity of the Beginning Experience. When Kathleen spoke her message was of action in preserving and furthering the ministry. I believed God chose her to be the director and gave her, daily, all that she needed for leading the Beginning Experience.

Next morning Father Ollie, their chaplain, and I left to drive west across Ireland to Sligo. On the journey we talked about the power of love and the power of letting go. He had been a missionary in Nigeria. After contracting malaria, he had come back to Ireland and worked in Family Life ministry. He lived letting go into abundance.

As we were driving along, I was telling him about Father Sebastian's suggestion of going to the monastic village of–and I took out my scrap of paper and spelled C-L-O-N-M-A-C-N-O-I-S-E. Father Ollie said, "There is the road sign right here for it." So we turned off and went the 20 km to it. What synchronicity!

That monastic village was filled with great Celtic crosses, many churches and two round towers. We viewed an excellent film giving its history. Saint Ciaran founded it on the banks of the Shannon River, which in the sixth century was a significant crossroad. The museum displayed the chalices and beautiful gold work done by these ancient monks whose lives were spent in prayer, work and art. The presentations of community life there rivaled any wax museum in the world. I could envision a day in the lives of those who were the folks who lived in that monastic village. They were families who centered their lives around the monastic rhythms of prayer and work. I pictured in my mind the monks singing the Divine Office, creating the beautiful art pieces, chiseling the Celtic crosses, building the round towers and constructing the churches and monastery. I was overjoyed about this unplanned detour on my pilgrimage.

Foremost on my "must do" list was to visit Athlone, where our Sister Benita Frances was born and raised. She was an important person in the history of the Beginning Experience. She was principal of Saint Cecilia's School in Dallas. Jo Lamia's sons attended that school at the time of the divorce of their parents. Jo was immobilized by her grief over her divorce and Sister Benita Francis, who recognized her grief, offered Jo a job as substitute for a teacher on maternity leave. Jo reluctantly agreed, "just until the end of the school year." The responsibility and her loving contact with the children started her healing. Twenty-seven years later, up to her death, she was still teaching Junior High math at Saint Cecilia's. I had visited with Sister Benita Francis before my trip and told her I hoped to visit her hometown of Athlone. She showed me a postcard of its castle and I actually saw it. Being in Athlone put me in touch with the root beneath the tree of the Beginning Experience.

I only spent a day in Sligo with the West of Ireland team, but in that short time I saw that they were living examples of Celtic hospitality. I was impressed with the vibrant faith of those people and especially of the young people. That evening, we attended the Beginning

Experience "Coping Program," one of the six weekly sessions for those newly separated or widowed. The topic was "living alone and loneliness." The talks were emotional. That session was the last of my short visit in Sligo. I was leaving for Derry, Northern Ireland, the next day.

The drive to Derry was a trip through history. On the way to Donegal Town, we saw the Famine Graveyard. The English had exported the corn grown in that area and had not left enough for the Irish. Thousands of farmers had gone to work houses and died there. They had been put into mass graves and covered with lime. Before that famine there had been 6,000,000 people in Ireland; after the corn and potato famine half the population emigrated or died leaving only 3,000,000 people. It didn't have to happen. The Irish had been terribly persecuted by the English–treated less than human. I reflected on the evil of greed and violent control and prejudice. I prayed to recognize these tendencies in myself and asked God to heal me.

I mentioned that terrible incident of the bloody conflict between the English and the Irish, because it shed light on the current situation in Ireland, in particular in Northern Ireland. Many of the Beginning Experience participants on the weekend and those who had attended the six week "Coping" sessions were widowed from the war that had gone on in their country. It was not just a Catholic vs. Protestant war, but a war more precisely between the English and the Irish. Participants on the Beginning Experience came from both sides of the conflict. They had put aside their animosities in order to move through grief, possibly caused by the "other side," to find resurrection together.

We arrived in Derry, Northern Ireland and went to the location where the Young People's Beginning Experience team was making massive preparations for the weekend. I observed the mountains of supplies for art projects for the teenagers whose parents were divorced or had died. What an enormous venture just to get all that together! What joy and love were shown by those volunteers as they prepared for the next day's retreat!

I had come especially to Derry to attend, as a participant, the Young People's Beginning Experience (YPBE). My friend, Bridie Gallagher, was the leader and power behind this ministry. It was because of her that I had come.

But before going I wanted to go to Linsfort to the Loreto retreat house. I also wanted to have a good visit with Sister Gertrude on the Derry team. So I did those two things during the day before going to YPBE.

My time at Linsfort was wonderful! We drove along the banks of Laugh (pronounced lock), Sevilley. The bright sunshine sent sparkles on the blue water. It was chilly but not cold. I arrived just in time for the closing Mass for a group of high school girls from Omagh Loreto School where Sister Anne, the retreat director, had been principal.

The Omagh students had planned the scripture readings for the Mass. The Old Testament reading was of Noah's Ark and the Rainbow. What a lovely coincidence for me with the L'Arche community whose spirituality had centered on the ark, place of refuge for the mentally handicapped people. The rainbow, promise of God's faithfulness, had been ever present at L'Arche. In that Mass, the past and present came together. I was thrilled to receive Communion there with that community. I loved the Irish hymns they sang. The altar was a large piece of gnarled driftwood.

After Mass, Sister Anne gave me a bedroom overlooking the beach. I sat in the bedroom and journaled and prayed. Using the walking stick she had given me I went down to the beach, sat on a rock and contemplated the glory of God in the immense ocean before me. I was surrounded by the sound of the waves and the wind.

The retreat house was something of a miracle in itself. The Loreto Sisters had bought it for £ 250 because it was in total disrepair and had spent £800,000 renovating it. Sister Anne had supervised the work. The man who kept the grounds had created a lovely Labyrinth, a meditation path in the form of a circular maze, which I could see out my window. Stain glass windows in a beautiful solarium depicted creation. The windows were created in memory of the 19 students of Omagh who were tragically killed in a 1998 massacre. They were killed after a peace agreement should have ended the war between the Protestants and Catholics. Sister Anne had been the Head Mistress of the school they attended and had taught some of them. Out of her love for her students she had created the solarium for the retreat center.

After my wee retreat I spent time with Sister Gertrude who had been on the Derry team. I had met her at the Houston International

Convention in 1990. My visit, our last one, was important to me. She spoke of having great devotion to Saint Therese of Liseux whose simple teaching of doing all for love had impressed her as a young girl. She had striven during her life to do all for love, to see God in all and to let God love each person through her.

I remember Sister Gertrude in Houston telling me that she thought the Incarnation and Redemption happened because Mary had said "yes" to God. Then she boldly told me that my "yes" to God had resulted in the creation of the Beginning Experience and the transformation of the lives of thousands of people. I was absolutely blown away by that comparison of my "yes" to Mary's "yes." Being with Gertrude again led me to think how obedience simply meant doing what was in front of one with joy. Gertrude's face was translucent, radiating her life, lived for love. She gave me her Birthday Card of the Transfiguration, the feast on which she had been born. The scripture quotation was 2 Cor. 3:18, "And we, with our unveiled faces, reflecting like mirrors the brightness of the Lord, all grow brighter and brighter as we are turned into the image that we reflect. This is the work of the Lord who is Spirit."

She finished our visit with a gesture meditation on abundance: the left hand pushes away the negative of the past; the right hand pushes away the negative of the future; open hands receive abundance. Then after putting hands together in a gesture of prayer, they open to receive loved ones, the world, the young, the starving, those in wars and violence. We ended by holding all in folded hands and breathing abundance into them.

Half-way through the meditation, I started becoming anxious knowing that I should have been "collected" 30 minutes earlier. I consciously gave my anxiety to God and, just as we finished the meditation someone came to get me.

Our goodbye was tender, knowing that we would not meet again on this earth. We said, "'til heaven." I truly carry Sister Gertrude in my heart and keep that Birthday Card in my Missal.

The Young People's Beginning Experience was at the "Peace and Reconciliation Center" in Derry, Northern Ireland. It had often been the venue for reconciliation between Northern Ireland and the IRA. The Dalai Lama and Nelson Mandela had conducted meetings on reconciliation and forgiveness there.

159

All of the young people had deep grief from personal losses from the endless war in Ireland. The talks given by the teenage team members were heart-wrenching, telling how the violence affected them. They told of the effects on them from suicide, murder, permanent disability, and divorce and separation from family.

The presentations were given in a big room with large windows, through which we could see blooming poppies. My small group was loving toward one another and toward me. One young man shared that he trusted totally in God, that God would never abandon him.

The closing was spectacular–a real expression of the Resurrection after the suffering and "dying" experienced by those young people. We stood outside around the edge of a large circle, inside of which was a mosaic of the world map. We released helium balloons and sang, "Shalom, shalom, shalom, 'til we meet again, shalom." I had a strong sense that we would meet again in heaven.

After a day at the Ulster/American Folk Museum at Omagh, we went to the walled city in Derry to the Cathedral, with magnificent stained glass windows, but most impressive to me was just outside the Cathedral. The statue of two tall, gaunt figures reaching with outstretched arms toward each other–almost touching. It depicted the struggle for, but never reaching, reconciliation. I decided to carry that image in my mind and to re-dedicate myself to forgiveness and reconciliation.

That evening we spent time at a wrap up and goodbye party before I departed next day. I was sad to be leaving these young people and their parents. The day I left Derry to go to Belfast, there was a bright rainbow and drizzle. I was going to see Pania, daughter of my long time New Zealand friend, Shirley. I had known her as a teen-ager in New Zealand and then I had seen her in Belfast in 1987 when she had a wee baby, Jesse. She had since divorced and was coping as a single mom.

I was delighted to see Pania, beautiful and quite mature looking, and her daughter Jesse, now six years old. I entertained Jesse with my photo album. She asked about each detail and seemed fascinated by the crucifixes. Pania and I laughed and talked about life in Christchurch, New Zealand and her mum and the family gathering the past year.

Pania's friend, Paul, was a fireman and a gourmet cook, artist and photographer. He was very "hang loose." He spoke of the violence of the bombings in Belfast and of the camaraderie among the firemen. Since the bombings have stopped, his work was more boring. I asked him about addiction to excitement. He told me that he wasn't a fireman for that, but for helping people and for the friendships. He came from Belfast and, after two very sad relationships, he found Pania.

I was wondering where I would sleep. The guest bed was a fireman's cot. I slept well, and when I awoke I saw a window into the life of a single mom. Pania and Jesse were eating their breakfast on high stools at a fold out table in the kitchen. Pania had her arms lovingly around Jesse. Jesse's art work was on display on a lovely board in the kitchen. She was quite artistic and was surrounded by a nurturing environment. I watched the gentle way that Pania brushed her hair and put it up in a bun because "today is ballet." Saturdays she went to Jazichu (a type of Karate) to learn discipline and to protect herself. She loved it. She dressed herself in her gray school uniform, black shoes, backpack and mauve warm jacket. She hugged me goodbye. Then Pania walked her to school – a five-minute walk around the corner.

I had brought Jesse a Russian toy of chickens pecking seeds. For Paul and Pania, I brought a large, bright butterfly, made in Mexico, to symbolize new life.

On the way to the airport, Pania and Paul drove along beside the shipyards where the Titanic had been built. The yellow rigs were still standing. The airport was a beautiful, modern silver building. We arrived in plenty of time, although at times I wondered if we would. I was thankful that I was able to visit them.

The short flight to London Gatwick Airport was about 20 minutes late. A man with a cell phone contacted Sandra, the one who had offered me hospitality when I was at the Leeds Conference. And, yes, she lived just minutes away from Gatwick. Again, I marveled at how little bits of synchronicity were showered on me all along my way on the trip and throughout my life.

After we arrived at Sandra's home, two Beginning Experience friends arrived from the Arondale/Brighton Team. We had a lovely meal and then the big surprise—my dear friend, Pauline Weber, had driven an hour and a half to come to see me. She taught during the day, and counseled in the evenings. Her last client cancelled, so she decided to drive over. I was overjoyed. She was eager to tell me about a study she had done of grief with L'Arche core members. She believed that all progress was because of the client-therapist relationship. She based her own counseling on that principle.

She loved Father Guy, who had contracted Parkinson's disease since she'd seen him. I had a chance to tell her some Guy stories about him driving and crashing his electric scooter at the monastery. Pauline left late for the long drive home. I treasured that visit with her, and her sacrifice to come to see me.

On the cool, dry day of my departure, I told Sandra how grateful I was for transitioning me from Ireland to England and then on to the flight home. I was pre-boarded to a bulkhead seat next to a lovely woman from Nigeria on her way to Charlotte, North Carolina, with her cuddly baby who was very quiet. As we took off, I thanked God with all my heart for His precious care of me each step of the journey. It had been a real pilgrimage.

The next day, October 24, feast of Archangel Raphael, I spent time just praying for and thanking God for each facet of the trip and asking Him to heal the wounds of His Wounded Healers of he Beginning Experience in that part of our world.

I went through my journal thinking of each one and each situation. I remembered all the angels of transport, hospitality, laughter, tears, comfort and storytelling.

The abundance of God's love was pressed down and overflowing.

CHAPTER 21

AFTERTHOUGHTS

In writing my memoirs, I have been surprised by the many "unknown-to-me" elements of my life. The abundance of my life, both tells the story of the Beginning Experience as the fruit of my life, and shows it as my teacher, directing me how to live my life. The Beginning Experience has taught me to be a reconciling person of peace and someone dedicated to non-violence.

One of the surprises in writing my story has been to see clearly the vibrant threads woven throughout my life.

The thread of "letting go" has jumped out at me. Wrenching separation started early in my life, from being weaned too young, to the trauma of going to first grade, to leaving treasured places and beloved people in my adulthood. My feelings of emptiness about having no home was a "river" underneath all and God healed that void for me.

God taught me in playful ways to let go: by taking the risk of using ink to sketch instead pencil, and by letting myself feel scary exhilaration by riding ocean waves. Of great importance, God gave me a flash of inspiration to let go of the power over Beginning Experience by deciding to have a decision-making board.

The thread of bountiful abundance came often as a result of God turning me around. I've laughed as I've written about God's doing the exact opposite of what I intended. My hasty decision to sample convent life in order to avoid a marriage proposal that I did not want to accept; my going to the *Happening*, after I resisted it, set in motion the whole sequence of events leading to the creation of the Beginning Experience; my writing Beginning Experience was the result of writing the Engaged Encounter; and deciding to work at Casa de Esperanza was because of a car wreck on the way to vacationing on Galveston Island.

I've smiled as I've seen synchronicity and convergence, like the serendipitous finding of my confirmation God-mother. In writing my story I have become more aware of and appreciative of my gift of intuition which helps me tune into and resonate with the feelings in another person.

A big "Ah ha" for me was seeing for the first time how deeply connected I am with the "spirit world." I have a strong awareness of my guardian angel, of Archangel Raphael, of my relatives and friends in Heaven, of precious Jo Lamia, of Uncle John (who mystically came to me) and under all is my unbreakable connection to God.

My home is God. And I am God's home. I have a personal friendship with God sustained by writing to God and then listening by writing down what God says to me.

My prayer is very physical: writing, riding the waves, sketching (as becoming one with) and swimming in the ocean of God's love.

In closing I invite you, beloved reader, to start your journey into yourself, by writing your story in a notebook or on the computer. I trust that you will be swept into a voyage of discovery, where you will see what is invisible to you and then begin to see the threads woven though your life, revealing a continuity and meaning that had escaped you before.

-30-

APPENDIX 1

WHAT IS THE BEGINNING EXPERIENCE?

It is a gentle process in which people who are widowed, divorced or separated are invited to pass through their grief and to gently close the door on the past in order to be transformed into a new life. It is an *experience* not an *encounter* (as was popular in the '70s). It is a gradual process focusing on passing through, not over or around, grief. The program is based on the solid theology that Christ lives, dies, and rises in each person.

There is a distinction between phases and method. Combined they form the process. So when I say "process," I am referring to both the phases and the method.

The first phase is looking at oneself and the last phase ends with reaching out to others. Between those phases the participants reflect in a personal way on their passage through the grief stages. They reflect on their trust of themselves, others and God.

The phases continue by helping the participants sort out their guilt. They offer an opportunity for forgiving and being forgiven. Finally, each person is invited to close the door on the past, to start anew, and to reach out to others. All is done in safety and with others who are going through their grief, too.

To achieve the phases, the method consists of three parts which are repeated throughout the weekend: listening to the personal life-story talks given by team members; private reflecting by participants; sharing in small groups. The small group is where a special bond with others is established. The method is what lends rhythm and flow to the weekend. Peace and joy are evident throughout.

What distinguishes this program from workshops is that it is "peer," like-to-like. The presenters and group leaders are themselves widowed, separated or divorced. This is what makes them peers. Therefore, they are not talking down to the participants from some professional viewpoint. They are peers, having experienced a grief similar to that of the participants, but who have been trained as ministers.

Jo Lamia and I knew that broken people can be made whole through this process which was discovered in her story.

After testing the process with several groups, this copyrighted program spread throughout the United States and Canada, and then was brought to Australia, New Zealand, Singapore, Great Britain and Ireland and recently it has started in Wales. There are 117 certified teams presenting the Beginning Experience on three continents.

Other satellite programs are in place. "Coping" provides weekly sessions for those newly singled again and could be a preparation for the core weekend program. After the weekend "Continued Beginnings" provides a follow through to the weekend.

In addition, but not the least, there are Beginning Experience programs for children, teen-agers and young adults.

For more information and to see the extent of the satellite programs, contact: www.beginningexperience.org.

APPENDIX 2

THE UNIVERSAL APPEAL OF THE BEGINNING EXPERIENCE

Although the Beginning Experience was started to meet a local need in the Dallas/Fort Worth area, it spread quickly and eventually went overseas. Of utmost concern was the answer to the question, "Are people in other cultures healed by its process?" (See Appendix: "What is the Beginning Experience?")

That led to other questions. "Do children, young people and young adults benefit from the same process?" "What are the lasting effects, through the years, for persons to cope and live fully?" "Are teams around the world faithful to our Vision and Mission by facilitating real grief resolution?" "Do those who have been through our program see themselves as participating in the suffering, death and resurrection of Christ as He lives in our world today?" "Is every team member truly peer, in that they have all personally experienced loss through separation, divorce or death?" And finally, "Are we all living the Vision of 'hurting people healed, transformed and free again to love themselves, others and God?'" I needed answers to these questions.

Chapters 19 and 20 are about the experiences that gave me the answers. We had already set up a simple structure of regions (Asia Pacific; Great Britain and Ireland; and North America) to provide communication and accountability. Every other year these regions held conferences. I attended some of those gatherings and then lived with team members afterwards. It was there that I found the answers to those questions. I saw first hand that the Beginning Experience had universal appeal and applicability.

APPENDIX 3

1. Daddy's father: Mack Stewart

2. Mama's mother: Josephine Eugenie Mouton Buchanan

3. Daddy's wedding picture, 1930, Wylie Stewart

4. Mama's wedding picture, 1930, Helen Buchanan Stewart

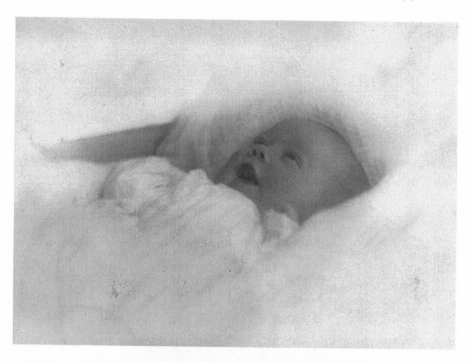

5. Josephine Stewart, as a baby, 1931

6. Daddy's Aunt Bessie Stewart

7. Jonie at four years of age

8. Jonie (R) at 16 years of age and Nancy Neil in Juarez, Mexico

9. Josephine at 20 in college

10. American novices in Belgium, 1955. I'm in the center as Soeur Raphael

11. Sister Raphael as Principal of Girls' Division of Bishop Dunne High School, 1964

12. Sister Raphael as assistant Principal of Girls' Division of Bishop
Dunne High School, 1966

13. Sister Josephine as Guidance Counselor of Bishop Dunne High School, 1968

14. Sister Josephine on staff of Saint John the Apostle Catholic Church,
Fort Worth Texas, 1973

15. Sister Josephine and Jo Lamia, working with the Beginning Experience, 1974

16. Jo Lamia, Co-founder of the Beginning Experience

17. Jo Lamia and Margaret's group on the Pilot Weekend in Christchurch, New Zealand, November 1979

18. Sister Josephine and Shirley's group on the Pilot Weekend in Christchurch, New Zealand, November 1979

19. Sister Josephine and 2 year old Daniel Brier on Coromandel sheep farm, 1982

20. John Dyksma, boot boy, and his sister Rosalie at peace rally, Christchurch, New Zealand. Their mother, Glenda has back to camera

21. Veronica and Noel, Christchurch, New Zealand

22. John Dyksma, age 28, Christchurch, New Zealand

23. Sister Josephine and guard dog Dumplin', Lake Jackson, Texas

24. Sister Josephine and Father Guy in Guatemala City, 1989

25. Little boy outside restaurant in Guatemala City, 1989

26. Woman with her children, who was selling melons and weaving on strap loom, on road to lake Atitlan, Guatemala, 1989

27. Maria and her children at the windows' camp outside Coban, Guatemala, 1989

28. Mama's last Christmas, 1990, with grandson Jim in foreground
and Daddy in background

29. L'Arche in Tacoma, Bill Downey hugging, with Les in background, 1995

30. Bill Downey portrait, 1996

31. Sister Christella, Spiritual Advisor of L'Arche in Tacoma, Washington, 1996

32. Irish Stepdancers from Young People's Beginning Experience (YPBE) Team in Derry, Northern Ireland, 1993

33. Daddy at picnic near Sandia Mountain, Albuquerque, New Mexico, Sister Josephine in background, 1998

34. The Briers in New Zealand in 2000. L-R Gerard(26), Kelly(27), Veronica(16), John and Anne, Robert(19), Brandon(23), above Daniel(21)

35. Mama and Daddy at their 50th Wedding Anniversary in Taos, New Mexico

APPENDIX 4

A. Ink Sketch of sheep shearing on Brier's farm on the Coromandel, February 1982

B. Pencil Sketch of Big Ceramic Pot with rain dripping on it, February 1982

C. Pencil Sketch of Kauri trees on the Coromandel in New Zealand, February 1982

D. Ink drawing of daisies on Mab's breakfast table, February 1982

E. Ink sketch of Wood Stove in Hermitage at Kennedy's Bay, April 1982

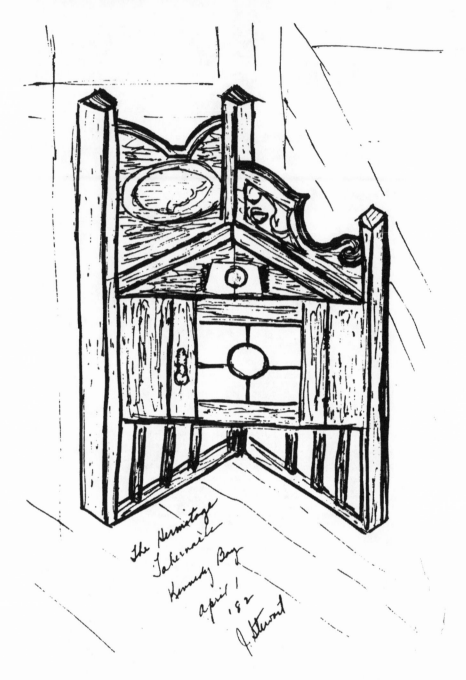

F. Ink sketch of Tabernacle in Chapel at Kennedy's Bay, April 1982

G. Ink sketch from Hermitage Porch, out over the Pacific, with
Pahutukawa Tree, April 1982

H. Ink sketch of gnarled trunk of Pahutukawa Tree on the Brier Farm, Easter, 1982

I. Ink sketch, from the bus, of first sight of peaks in Fiorland, South
Island, New Zealand, July 1982

J. Ink sketch, out my window in the hotel, of the Remarkables, July 1982

K. Ink sketch of Queenstown and the Remarkables from the top in the Skyline
Coffee Shop, July 1982

L. Ink sketch of Ioa Needle, Island of Maui, Hawaii, November 1982

M. Ink sketch of little Church Steeple framed by Live Oaks, Grand Couteau
Louisianan, May 1983

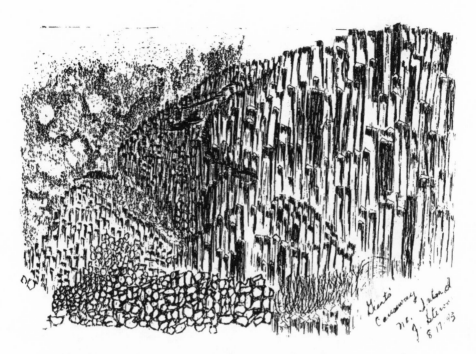

N. Ink sketch of Giants' Causeway, Northern Ireland, August 1993

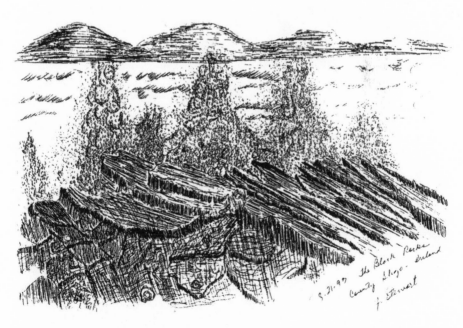

O. Ink sketch of waves crashing on Black Rocks, Sligo, West of Ireland, August 1993

P. Ink sketch from sitting in field of Heather, of Bailey Lighthouse near Dublin, Ireland, August 1993

Sister Josephine is a native Texan, living in Wichita Falls. Her life starts in 1931 during the Great Depression and spans the changes in society and in the Catholic Church during the 20th century. She entered the Sisters of Saint Mary in 1953 and lived through the transformation from the traditional life of a nun, through Vatican 2 and into involvement in social issues.

Her unique personal history, her resonance with Jo Lamia's life story, and God's inspiration led her to create the Beginning Experience and to guide its growth. She has seen it cycle through the Christ mystery of suffering, dying and rising to bring hope to separated, divorced and widowed people around the world.

Made in the USA
San Bernardino, CA
17 December 2013